GW00599592

THERE'S A RAINBOW ON THE RIVER

DEDICATION

With Love
To My Fabulous Family

Concepter Bale

There's a Rainbow on the River

AUSTIN MACAULEY

A CIP catalogue record for this title is available from the British Library.

ISBN 978 1 84963 017 7

www.austinmacauley.com

First Published (2012)
Austin & Macauley Publishers Ltd.
25 Canada Square
Canary Wharf
London
E14 5LB

Printed & Bound in Great Britain

ACKNOWLEDGEMENTS

My most grateful thanks to MR DAVID CROFT for his generous permission to include dialogue from the television series ALLO ALLO, and to the
STAMP DESIGN CENTRE
©ROYAL MAIL GROUP LTD for their permission to include the stamp and logo for my story of RJ Mitchel.

I also wish to acknowledge the following companies with many thanks for their kind co-operation in tracing music and lyrics, and giving permission for the following song excerpts:

RAINBOW ON THE RIVER
Words and Music by LOUIS ALTER and PAUL FRANCIS WEBSTER © 1936 (renewed) EMI FEIST CATALOG, INC. and WEBSTER MUSIC CO. Exclusive Print Rights for EMI FEIST CATALOGUE, INC. Controlled and Administered by ALFRED MUSIC PUBLISHING CO., INC.
All Rights Reserved

WARNER/CHAPPEL MUSIC LIMITED
"LITTLE DONKEY" – composer ERIC BOSWELL
"BELLS ARE RINGING" – composers BETTY COMDEN, ADOLPH GREEN, JULE STYNE
"I GET A KICK OUT OF YOU" – composer COLE PORTER

EMI MUSIC PUBLISHING LIMITED
Of 27 Wrights Lane, London W8 5SW ("EMI")
"OVER THE RAINBOW" words and music by E.HARBURG and HAROLD ARLEN © 1938, reproduced by permission of EMI FEIST CATALOG INC,
LONDON W8 5SW.

Dear Reader,

This will not apply to everyone but because the book has such a huge message of JOY, it can, for some people, be tiring to read.

This is a NORMAL and completely harmless reaction, if a little strange. If we just put it away for a little while and pick it up again later, we gradually get used to it.

It would be such a pity to give up reading it before the last page and miss what will be for all of us one day
A HAPPY ENDING.

P.S. And why a CAVALRY SWORD in the cover design?
To show us how to sort out this wonderful world.

THE CAVALRY'S COMING...

PROLOGUE

It is a well known fact that Romany Gypsies have an extra kind of perception for which there could be a logical explanation. In the history of civilisation up to this last century there has always been a class system where peasantry married peasantry and educated people married partners from their own background so that a divided way of living became natural. As we know, apart from odd instances, no princess or 'class' person married a peasant and with travel virtually impossible for poorer people before the railways, multi-heritage must have been the exception to the rule.

This century the system is fast changing; the class distinctions disappearing rapidly, so I believe we will have, quite soon, people who will have a higher intelligence than ever before. Babies are being born now with backgrounds like my little grandson, who has a heritage of LATVIA, IRELAND, SCOTLAND, ROMANY, PEASANT and CLASS, and with such heredity, how can these children have anything else but the edge on previous generations?

It is therefore possible that the extra bit of insight on the part of the gypsies, could be attributable to the fact that a large number of Romanys were taken prisoner by the Lords of Romania and made slaves, so that many half-class and half-peasant babies are likely to have been born. By the time their descendents had travelled through countries occasionally marrying people with other backgrounds from their own, multi-heritage may well have begun on a substantial scale with the Romanys. My belief is this has had confirmation in such a happy experience but first I had to visit...

BRIGADOON

Brigadoon is a mythical village in SCOTLAND that can only appear for one day every century, the reason being, someone, (probably multi heritage) had seen that if they only lived for one day every hundred years, they would not catch the chain reaction of the evils of the period; for today, a chain reaction is what we have.

When we are unhappy others get to know – that makes them unhappy and the more unhappy we are the more unhappy decisions we are likely to make. English newspapers and television talk repeatedly of illness, vice, and crime, and although this is sometimes necessary and can't be avoided, it will often give the impression that things can only get worse. I know there are programmes of education and comfort, but once the seeds of insecurity are sown the resulting chain reaction is inevitable, because the more we concentrate on negative things the more negative they will become.

With a background of gypsy and dress designer, it stands to reason that travelling round to auctions and producing musical shows I have found the right lifestyle for my heritage. The personalities who run the auctions are full of fun. Laughter generates JOY, so auction day must help to balance out the adverse chain reaction.

One day I bid for a box of odds and ends. It contained two lovely ornaments; someone, who usually sorts the good things out had accidentally put them in the wrong box, mine being worth only a few shillings. So unusual – as this crew is always very efficient. I phoned HARRY the auctioneer, but he said that the ornaments were their mistake and he would compensate the owners. The ornaments, with a few more things that it had been ordained that I should come across, went to another beautiful person who needed them badly for her shop. She gave me FORTY-FIVE pounds! My cry to God for a holiday answered, I set off for Surrey to stay the night with a newly widowed friend before travelling on.

At my destination I found a lady who, at eighty-six years old can still come high in the glamour stakes and can tackle a game of scrabble at ten o'clock at night, and win! She has, too, the stimulating tendency to stop people from concentrating on their aches and pains. This power is needed at her senior citizens club. I've no doubt it has been given her, along with wonderfully preserved looks, to break the chain reaction of too many negative telly programmes and news bulletins that are swinging around.

She had planned to buy a SAINSBURYS STRAWBERRY SPONGE CAKE WITH BUTTER CREAM FILLING for our tea, but was forestalled by winning, in a raffle, a SAINSBURYS STRAWBERRY SPONGE CAKE WITH BUTTER CREAM FILLING. After I had asked her for a book for my friend NATHAN, who collects show business biographies, she insisted I take my smart shoes (which I had intended leaving with her). 'You might need them,' she said, I carried on my way to LONDON.

In the coach station café I met a lady who was single and lonely. She had the vivacity and the power to brighten up any gathering she was in, but she didn't realise her own potential, so I felt it important to point this out to her. When ERICA had gone I felt quite worried about her and remembered that I hadn't got her address, so went back to find her before going on to the underground train.

On the platform a young girl came up to me and said, "WOULD YOU LIKE MY RUNABOUT TICKET? I COULD ONLY USE IT ONCE AND NOW I DON'T NEED IT ANY MORE."

I was on a very tight budget and if I hadn't gone back to find ERICA, I wouldn't have been in the right place at the right time. I asked the coach people for a ticket to anywhere, as far as the money would take me. My nomadic personality would be quite satisfied provided the journey was long.

On the bus I sat next to a charming young man from Africa who was going to university. When we arrived at Newcastle, I was duly escorted to a train to where an inexpensive 'Bed and Breakfast' could be found, but had no success though in finding a place vacant, so I took off in a different direction. At the station I asked a lovely girl if she knew of somewhere to stay and she said:

"I DO BED AND BREAKFAST," (she had just returned from the same road that I had searched, and where she had been walking her dogs), so promptly drove us to her home where I met DANIEL, who had spent years as a YOUTH CLUB LEADER. It was DANIEL'S idea to go to SCOTLAND and he told me of the tourist office where I could get details of accommodation.

The young man in the office was very helpful, and I was given the address of a lady who made me so welcome in her beautiful home. Over the teacups though, I realised straight away that she was so distressed by all the sadness in the world and not a little alarmed by it, and I felt dreadfully concerned for her.

By this time it was Wednesday and only two more days left. I seemed to be driven into worrying about all the people I had met and my heart was racing with a strange inner excitement. I know now that this was nothing to be alarmed about, but hopes of a relaxing holiday were fast disappearing. The disappointment was awful, having looked forward to the first holiday for years and instead was preoccupied with the world's misery, and the poverty that the young man from AFRICA must be only too aware of. Heart banging like a drum, I went into a Catholic Church. Never been inside one before – how light and bright it was – but wept when realising how the week was going by and how exhausted I felt.

At the tourist office a poster said…

HIGHLAND TOUR, TEN O'CLOCK

But it was then ten-thirty. Just as I was thinking that I had missed it all, a young man came in to say that the "minibus was ready now" having had engine trouble. So I got in with five other people all travelling alone, and from different parts of the world, to be transported off to the HIGHLANDS to laugh and to eat haggis on the mountainside. Such beauty of scenery I have never seen before; the rowan berries against the clear blue sky and the sound of bagpipes filling the air. My companions were all such delightful people, who never once referred to anything that could mar our day. They were all generators of LIGHT.

We were resting in an old-fashioned village inn when the young man who organised the tour asked us why we had chosen to come to SCOTLAND. Still struggling with our language, KIA from JAPAN said...

"I HAD INSPIRATION OF QUIET JOY."

When it came to my turn, I told them of the ornaments and how the many coincidences that I had been experiencing lately were something to do with LOVE and JOY, and how the fare was FORTY-FOUR pounds and I had been given FORTY-FIVE.

In the evening there was a SCOTTISH CEILIDH (this is a traditional social evening with fiddles and dancing, singing and laughter). The tour young man knew that I may be short of money, so he produced a ticket and I was so thankful that I had been made to take the shoes.

There I met LUDVIG, who, in the course of the evening happened to remark that his homeland GERMANY had recovered faster from the war than the conquering country, because the class distinctions were absent. A pattern that later became consistently relevant.

In the night, unable to sleep, the banging heart and drumming in my ears were too loud to be able to ignore. It became imperative that I write a note and leave it for my hostess and simply had no choice but thought what can I write it on? Then I spotted the book I had taken for NATHAN, so tore out the fly leaf and wrote that the coincidences were too frequent to be accident, and that the extraordinary things that were happening (and I have had to condense so much) mean that nothing harmful is going to happen to this lovely world that can't be rectified one day, only that it is time for 'ACTION STATIONS'.

The next day I returned to Newcastle and DANIEL and told him of the astonishing incidents leading up to my holiday. Just in time he saw me onto the coach for London. Settling in the seat, thought I could have a rest and forget it all for a little while, having had my fill of unusual things and felt a little good old normality would be a good thing, but it was not to be.

Our JOSH, a friend who had lived nearby had recently died. An explanation was beginning to dawn on me that could give SADIE his wife, great comfort. I knew that I must write to her straight away, but what on? Immediately the bus hostess dropped two paper bags onto the floor. I told SADIE to look out for any unusual things; like the time daughter ELLA won the CARNIVAL BINGO, believing JOSH would try to contact her.

On my return I asked a friend "HOW DID SADIE GET ON AT THE CARNIVAL LAST NIGHT?" to be told that she had won the ALL OVER CUP!

A few days later I received a letter from ERICA, (coach station remember?) to say that she had had her photo taken to go into a TIME CAPSULE.

GOOD HEAVENS! Of course! Suddenly the pieces fell into place. I had experienced one lovely day... ONE PERFECT DAY IN THE HIGHLANDS OF SCOTLAND AWAY FROM THE CHAIN REACTION OF ALL THE CARES IN THE WORLD, LIKE A TIME WARP...

BRIGADOON!

In the light of events that followed there can be no doubt that there is an existence parallel with ours, a DREAMLIKE state where we can speak to the subconscious mind of people like the hostess who dropped the bags, the lady who bought the cake, and the auction crew who 'slipped up' with the ornaments.

There is something different in the multi-heritage mind which makes coordination more possible than in previous generations. Somehow the people in the story have, with their goodness, generated the right conditions for the people in the 'Dimension' to contact us, and have the destiny to alter the adverse CHAIN REACTION in some way.

KIA, the Japanese young man, showed us a lovely exercise; perhaps it is his job to teach it, or DANIEL may have some young person in his club, who will need his encouragement to become one of the new generation to reverse this unhappy 'merry go round' we are on. Life is eternal, we have to 'do it all again' with a more evolved intelligence and when we have got ourselves organised we will save this wonderful world and literally

'REACH FOR THE STARS'.

On the day after my return from Scotland I went off to a

TRADITIONAL OLDE TYME FAYRE

The stalls manned by people in costume with musicians and street entertainers were set against the 'backdrop' of the old Abbey town like some fairy tale. Halfway up the high street, displayed in a shop window right out on its own, a lovely big painting of an old TRAIN in full steam which I have learned since was THE FLYING SCOTSMAN. Underneath the words

'WELCOME BACK'

It was weeks before I realised its significance.

That evening I noticed the quickening heart rate experienced during the trip and was compelled to write. It didn't worry me in the least, although my metabolism must have been doing 'double time'. Afterwards I saw that I had written a note to my friend SADIE to say that JOSH had put a little dog in RAY's garden so that when she hears it yap at dusk she will think of him. He said too that she might forget him so when she hears the little dog will be reminded.

Sometime before, RAY, who is a postman and lives next door to us and a few doors away from JOSH's home, along with his dear ZOE helped finance our first stage show.

He had a little pekingese dog who used to yap in the garden at dusk. It was an unusual sound; she would leave a little interval between each single bark. It was as though she was answering a signal that we were unable to hear.

RAY wondered if she could hear another dog somewhere. No one minded really as she was a dear little thing but it used to worry him. When she died TILLY was sorely missed as she had been with them for years and years. They replaced her with a collie thinking it would be quieter but soon realised their mistake as she needed more room.

A few days after, on his round, RAY just happened to meet a farmer who needed a dog and was glad to give 'BABS' a home. Within days circumstances changed too in little FIDO'S life bringing him into ours and 'lo and behold' if he didn't yap in EXACTLY THE SAME WAY AS TILLY HAD! It was as though she had never gone.

Everyone was 'tickled pink' at poor old RAY being clobbered with it again, so we all laughed together as FIDO is the dearest little thing as TILLY was, and RAY does know now that no one minds.

On the piano was a tape recording of a performance of our first show, 'PANTOMANIA'. Although we did many productions after, that was always for JOSH a favourite. When I reached over to get more paper, I accidentally knocked it off.

PLOP! It fell right into my

DOG'S BOWL!

Next evening my husband, ALEX, an avid CB Radio enthusiast, was working out the locations of some of his radio contacts with his map, and at the same time chanting out the names of towns in WALES that I had travelled through while on a coach trip with his auntie, who had shortly before passed away, (or so we thought).Then he announced that he was going to cycle over to see her house (he was hoping her lovely garden hadn't been neglected I expect). I had said nothing about the towns and he was not aware of where auntie and I had visited.

The next day I began to wonder, so being short of notepaper I took out the front page of an old book to use to write a note to SADIE thinking it would make her laugh to tell her of ALEX's trip so soon after he had been talking about the towns that auntie and I had visited.

Afterwards I noticed that I had written on the page with the caption…

'THE WINGED HORSE'.

ALEX had worn the red beret of the AIRBORNE SOLDIER in the war, and PEGASUS is the AIRBORNE emblem and his CB code name...

As everyone will know, PEGASUS is a WINGED HORSE from Greek mythology.

It was during the same week that I wrote a document explaining the theory of MISERY being the cause of adverse behaviour. My memory is hazy and was not conscious of it until afterwards. It was the first time anything like it had happened to me and was realising most definitely that without any shadow of a doubt people don't die.

The basic theory is, we have an inner capability to generate mental power. We store it like a battery does. When we are happy our positive level rises, when we are miserable our positive level goes down and our negative level rises.

Now if our JOY power goes down below the halfway mark we begin to make bad decisions or can feel unwell.

The lower our JOY level becomes, the less we are able to pull ourselves out of it, but when our positive level is well stocked up our decisions are likely to be the right ones and its impossible to be disagreeable or selfish.

Once the battery is full negatively it has to be discharged in some negative way. But when we are in crowds and all are happy as on NEW YEARS EVE in TRAFALGAR SQUARE for instance; the generator goes round faster because a lot of people are cheering with JOY together.

This will explain why a few people have to get into the fountains as our joy capacity can become a bit full and the cold water gets it back to a comfortable level. Some of us haven't had enough joy as a general thing to get used to it on a large scale and stretch our capability to contain it, so the fountains come in handy.

The trouble is that once we have discharged the battery in an adverse way, the ensuing misery we suffer when we realise how awful we have behaved RECHARGES THE BATTERY and off we go again. There is one big loophole in this though and I've tried and tested it many times since learning of it. When someone is suffering from an overfull misery 'battery charge', COMPASSION on the part of someone will NEUTRALISE it.

None of this is going to surprise anyone but what may not be widely known is that when a source of misery STOPS we have a little bit left in the battery still to burn out which is like a concentrated dose. For a time, until it's all gone, we can be our own worst enemy or feel unwell for a short time.

So if we have lost someone dear to us then our 'battery' will have a negative charge.

When we realise that our loved ones are safe and alive our misery charging STOPS, leaving a little left still to burn out. For a short time we can be irritable like saying something hurtful to the ones we love the best, so out of character, and afterwards think, "What made me say that?" (our personalities in REVERSE).

It is important for us to realise that there can be a lapse before the misery 'backlog burn out' sets in, this can vary according to how long we have been worrying. If we don't understand what is happening to us we can prolong it, but it goes away in 'no time' if we do and don't worry about it.

There are many who know subconsciously that we don't die and so can't suffer from BACKLOG TRAUMA as severely as others, not having generated misery about it. More will be explained about this later.

So when I realised that our darling JOSH and my parents were very much around, my fears STOPPED, and instead of being deliriously happy I woke up one morning thoroughly out of sorts and scared, and all the opposite way round.

Now that I understand the reason, there was no need for alarm. My own GOLDEN DAY has dawned and can laugh right merrily, as the world will when its MISERY BACKLOG has run out, but that morning I was very unhappy.

I had left my motorbike at the garage, so decided to catch a bus and bring it home. Super people run the garage; I thought that if I could get over there I would find friendship.

Before leaving I became unusually aware of colourful things around the kitchen. It was as though red, orange, yellow and green were shooting out at me like psychedelic colours do. The taped music that was playing seemed to synchronise and I began to associate the tunes with people who had left us. I absentmindedly took a blue ribbon from a drawer and tied it round my hair. Can you imagine anything more unlikely – being fifty-six and practically living in a crash helmet? At the same time the music played on.

With legs so shaky I had to hold the fence to stay upright, I set off down the lane.

It had been raining. In a field reaching exactly from hedge to hedge complete as though it was painted, a perfect RAINBOW.

When I arrived at the garage DAVID who runs it could see that something was wrong. He said...

"COME AND HEAR MY TAPE OF DANCE MUSIC."

He and his wife DORA dance beautifully and are such lovely people and I learned that everyone involved in this experience are all kind.

Colours were still shooting out at me in the shop. The blue reminded me of ADELE who had left us three years before. At Christmas I had made a dolly for her little girl and had put blue flowers on a blue dolly, a thing I never do. Usually the flowers are contrasting.

On the rack was a tool of some sort attached to a BLUE card. There were several, the brand name CHARLES. The name repeated on cards all along the shelf.

CHARLES CHARLES CHARLES CHARLES...

ADELE's husband is named CHARLES.

When the music started it consisted of all the tunes that had associations with friends who had left us to join the Dimension that so many of us have not been aware of until now.

There was one odd one out though. It was ages before I remembered that it had been sung by a friend who is in the Dimension too and was responsible for producing a carnival float that was called:

'THE END OF THE RAINBOW'.

It was six months after before I realised the connection between the colours and the rainbow, and even longer before it dawned on me how it was done.

On the following Sunday, the sky was flawlessly blue. Flying in circles were hundreds of seagulls and way above exactly over my head was a big plane forging along through the centre. The effect was breathtaking in its beauty.

Long ago and far away when I lived on the Norfolk coast, a well-known wild life artist stayed with us when he was illustrating his bird books. My mother did 'bed and breakfast' and he preferred our little cottage to the posh hotel. For some time I came across his work in all sorts of mediums; a chopping board, pictures and books, a painting in someone's house and a friend who knew him.

In the light of all that's happened since, I am sure that my mother knew that I was inevitably going to be lonely and unhappy for a short time. Aware that the thermals were going to be right for the seagulls she knew that I would be reminded of her and my childhood home when I saw them, and was able to make sure that I was in the garden hanging out the clothes to dry just at the right moment, when my young friend LUKE would be walking by, to cheer me up as he always does.

Important Footnote:

The following notes will not apply to everyone, I mention them only so as to reassure if people react as sensitively as myself. I found that in the early days of this experience I was unable to read the book without a kind of dazed feeling.

After a couple of chapters found that I would have to put it away as it was sort of exhausting and the burning face thing would return. Heart flutters too, a bit like novelists describe when people fall in love. I would also have a vague kind of dreamy sensation, like we can have with flu or measles when we were a kid. This soon goes away once we understand that odd feelings are NORMAL. The light-headedness doesn't matter once we realise what it is.

As time went on it disappeared and now I have no trouble at all and can read the book to my heart's content.

Of course this discomfort does not apply to everyone as there are so many books on the market now and some of us will not be too surprised. It's a bit like learning to sing, our throats are like stiff elastic that with exercises stretch a little every time we do them until they can open up to their full potential.

So it is with our JOY capacity, we have to get used to JOY gradually until it is sort of stretched big enough to contain it. So if discomfort is felt when reading this, if one just puts it away until another day the problem will gradually fade as we get used to it. It is only because we haven't understood these feelings before that the world has had to wait so long for the SUNRISE.

When I saw the big aircraft on the day of the seagulls I was reminded of CLIFF who flew one for a well known airline. It was three days after he died that I suddenly knew what was wrong with his son who was then in Dartmoor Prison.

As English people know, Dartmoor is just about the 'end of the line'. GLEN, such an endearing personality, baffling magistrates and doctors alike, as a tiny boy would do such colourful things. He was quite small when his grandmother lifted the lid of the piano only to find all the keys missing! (Of course he put them all back). To take him out to tea was all best forgotten.

His mother NANCY had been a dancer and had met CLIFF while they were both appearing in variety theatre; she as a contortion and sister act and he as comic feed and impersonator. Half-Swedish and half-English, ex-public school and RAF bomber pilot, for all that, CLIFF's time in show business was of the highest importance.

After a couple of years he decided to return to the airforce feeling that it would be a safer profession and flying big transport planes, but the kind of personality he was must have missed the challenge and excitement that is inevitable when the entertainment world is one's living.

Being in the wrong lifestyle can develop a misery battery charge as everyone knows, so seven years later things went wrong for them. NANCY brought the children back home from Germany and bravely brought them up alone, although she had her mother's help, had to go to secretarial college to start a new career. Meanwhile GLEN's little naughtiness became more colourful and serious.

Psychiatrists knew nothing about the years and years of training in the ballet or of the tremendous natural talent NANCY has, as like CLIFF she is multi-talented. All they knew was that she had been married to an RAF Officer and was in the civil service.

One night three days after I heard that CLIFF had died I was puzzling my brains to try to work out why such an intelligent and well-loved personality could be in Dartmoor. The effect on our darling NANCY was beginning to tell.

I wrote to a friend who is in the prison service to say, 'IF ONLY WE COULD UNDERSTAND WHAT GLEN IS TRYING TO CONVEY TO US.'

Then suddenly I knew…

On the bottom like a postscript I wrote:

'I'VE GOT IT! PRAY I'LL HAVE THE COURAGE TO TELL GLEN THE THEORY OF A LITTLE BOY WHO NEVER SAW HIS MOTHER DANCE.'

I have no doubt that his father heard his son's cry, and was able to directly say the clue, as that night, I could hear the word clearly go through my head;

'ENTERTAINER.'

He had never seen her entertain, she taught our lovely chorus girls but he was in prison then.

Had they stayed in show business for a while longer the boy and not the little girl, as one would expect, (although like her parents beautiful and multi-talented didn't have any problems) would have seen her rehearse and copied, and got his little act up a treat. One could say, how can it be that simple? An oak tree has a very simple beginning and a child's misery can be well away at a very early age.

GLEN was entertaining the world before he could speak, and misunderstood it himself, and a child's misery once charged means that it must be discharged in some negative way. Feeling guilty and ashamed of how he's carried on RECHARGES THE BATTERY so off he'll go again, round and round getting worse and worse.

When he had the explanation for what began his vicious circle, GLEN was able to get a grip on life.

A little while after her granddaughter sent a request letter to a popular television programme which was picked out of 170,000 for NANCY to appear.

She was enchanting and GLEN proudly switched on. Both he and NANCY have had such courage and I knew then that they would both survive to know happiness again.

AT THE TIME OF WRITING

It is nine years since I noticed coincidence for the first time. My daughter was working in a post office when they used to advertise with pictures of village post offices. I needed a picture to brighten a room, so she brought an out-of-date one home.

It was one of W---- ----S---- My Mother had often talked of the place, her post office savings book was stamped S----- so I was attached to it but thought no more.

A little while after when in a furniture store some lovely piano music was playing. I asked the young manager where I could buy it as it was super stuff.

He said, "ITS ME ACTUALLY," and went on to explain that he had made the recording with a famous orchestra in the hopes of getting it commercialised.

He kindly offered to make a recording of it and wouldn't even let me pay for the tape.

Some weeks later I heard from him to say that the original had been stolen and the recording he had made was the only one he had. (The record company probably had a copy, but would have been costly).

I took a sick friend out to tea one day. It was during one of my hard-up periods and just managed the price knowing that I would be a little short for the rest of the week.

Returning home I found a banknote in the hedge; no one claimed it. This just covered the cost of the tea.

Then there was the time I rode over a children's pedestrian crossing. The crossing keeper was well in his rights to be furious, so next day I wrote a written apology and changed my route to give it to him.

As I cut across country through isolated lanes to get back onto the right road I came upon a young man who had come off his motorbike.

Then I began to notice that if one did the Christian thing, one would always be in the right place at the right time. The pattern became so frequent that I lost count.

One day I needed a Hoover ring. The market stall lady was short of change, so rather than inconvenience her with my ten pound note, said that I would call back later. On the ground further along, found one in the road. A couple of weeks later found another a bit larger so I picked it up, wouldn't have bothered if I hadn't found the other one.

I make DOLLIES for a shop. A little girl fell in love with one, probably because they are based on the costumes from our shows. I promised to make her one for her birthday. This dolly was becoming very important to her.

I left it till the last minute, two days to go confident that it would be done in time, when the driving ring on the sewing machine snapped.

I rushed down to the shop where they stock the parts but the rings were sold out. I met her daddy who added, "Not to worry," but we both knew that disappointment was going to be great. Decided to get off to the nearest sewing machine shop fourteen miles away and was donning motorbike gear when I remembered the ring I had found in the road.

IT FITTED FINE.

It is most important that they are totally fair so they have to be careful how much they influence things. Nothing can come out right unless all is completely 'above board'.

They know that I must find some money to get this message circulating round the world.

Dental treatment clashed with an MOT test so I had a very expensive time. (Ministry of Transport safety check on the bike).

One jumble sale morning there was, stuck out in front, a pair of tiny shoes, donkeys' years old. It is so rare to find anything so valuable now as such things are so sought after. With a few more little things to sell I just had enough to pay for both bike and teeth.

Shortly after the bike packed up (being seventeen years old) and I developed toothache again. DAVID the super mechanic got this 'gypsy' back on the road again in a couple of hours and the dentist sorted once more. But of course, I was back to 'square one'.

Off jumbling the following Saturday, and what did I find but ANOTHER tiny pair of shoes, same period, same little pointed toes, same buckles.

They were a little more worn so there was an old handbag too. Instead of having to make dollies and teddies, was able to get on with this.

I never knew my grandmother, as she died before I was born and I never knew what she looked like. A year before, TONY, a cousin, had sent a photo of her that I never knew existed. On her knee was Uncle George, TONY's father, and by her side, my mother.

One morning I had the impulse to look at it and what did I see peeping out from under her long skirt?

A PAIR OF TINY SHOES WITH BUCKLES!

My mother said that she had tiny feet, size three I think.

We have a beautiful picture embroidered by my mother. Its subject is CHRIST KNOCKING AT A DOOR.

Its glass was broken, so I kept it in a plastic bag for years as I couldn't afford a new frame and was unable to find a second-hand one to fit.

One day while walking down town the day before refuse collection, opposite, a lady picked something up and put it down again.

I crossed over and saw that it was a picture. In the corner were the words:

RONALDSON PHOTOGRAPHERS NORWICH.

The name of the people who had owned it was PARSONS, (PARSON is an English name for an ordained minister).

My brother's name is RONALD, and I had just heard from his son to say that he was soon to be ordained into the CHRISTIAN CHURCH, and we had lived near, and had associations with NORWICH.

They must have known I go down that way and on that side of the street every week, and at the same time, the day before refuse collection. Having searched for something suitable, I think my mother simply suggested to someone's subconscious mind to throw it out, and then got the lady to pick it up so that I would cross over to see what she had been looking at.

The frame fitted OF COURSE

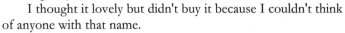

ALEX came in with a brand new MUG with a rude joke on it. I had it in a corner on the piano, out of sight where it stayed forgotten.

When at a bazaar I saw a lovely MUG. It looked shiny and new and was so pretty. On it was written the name NANCY.

I thought it lovely but didn't buy it because I couldn't think of anyone with that name.

I see NANCY often, we are such close friends and I've known her for years. It is extraordinary to forget her name.

She has lovely taste – the mug would have looked in keeping with her tiny cottage and would have given her such pleasure. Later on, realising this, I unhappily tried to think of some way of getting hold of it, hoping desperately that some miracle might get it into the following Saturday's jumble sale being held in the same hall. After all, some very extraordinary things were happening.

At nine o'clock I donned motorbike gear ready to go when I couldn't find the keys. Searched everywhere, getting 'strung up' and distressed, because NANCY didn't get her mug as I had forgotten her name and realising that 'someone' had gone to a lot of trouble to get it there. Without the bike keys. I couldn't go, (Later found them in an old coat). I looked up to the piano hoping still that I had left them on there. Right out on its own on the corner was perched,

THE NAUGHTY MUG!

Knowing nothing about the mug or the lost keys, ALEX had unconsciously picked it up and put it down again. JUST WHERE IT WAS MEANT TO GO intending to cheer me up, which it did right merrily. She can have that one instead.

The original mug <u>did</u> turn up again ages after but it is another story in itself and will have to wait until another time.

When I am puzzled about something they will sometimes use an old nursery rhyme, in which will be a clue.

All the stories are in proper sequence but I was not sure if I had got the picture frame one in the right order. Should it have gone in before the shoes? I wondered, when ALEX came in with;

"I'VE CHOPPED SOME STICKS FOR NANCE." (For her fire).

"THEY'RE IN THE GREENHOUSE."

Doesn't the old rhyme go:

"ONE, TWO, BUCKLE MY SHOE
THREE, FOUR, KNOCK ON THE DOOR
FIVE, SIX, PICK UP STICKS."

Out one day a friend said to me, "What was the name of that place in SCOTLAND that only came to life for one day every hundred years?"

He had entered a quiz show the night before and had been unable to answer the question.

On returning home and switching on the television, across the screen the words...

BRIGADOON BRIGADOON BRIGADOON...

The name came up again, on tape, radio and the telly, in the following few days.

I have another wise and sweet friend JILL who has the habit of saying

"WE'RE NOT IN THE DRIVING SEAT."

Meaning to trust in GOD in things. She calls me CON as others do, but sometimes makes little adjustments for fun, like CONTESSA or CONESTA, drawing attention to my name I realise now, with a list she had made of a lot of Christian names beginning with CON.

One day on television, a young man was teaching deaf children. He told them to 'concentrate', then mimed going to sleep and driving a car vigorously.

They guessed,

DREAM.

Later during a local news programme an inspector of police was worried about the increasing crime rate in this area and was puzzled and concerned at not being able to pinpoint the cause. It struck me that he was a very sincere sort of chap. He had in the studio a row of cars, which he was using to illustrate all the different confidence tricks with them. Each one had the number plate

CON 1, CON 2, CON 3, CON 4.

I think there were five, can't be certain if there were more as it is days before I realise the significance of these things.

I had been worried about how to circulate the theory with the MISERY CAUSES, ADVERSE BEHAVIOUR, and had no idea where to start. Its clear now though, there can be no doubt that this remarkable thing <u>has</u> happened, and the people in the dreamlike dimension have found a way to let us know things to our advantage.

And the message?

"CONCENTRATE, THE PEOPLE IN THE 'DREAM' ARE IN THE DRIVING SEAT. SEND THE BRIGADOON STORY AND THE MISERY VERSUS JOY THEORY TO CHIEF INSPECTOR G... (DEPUTY).

I know its astonishing, but then all new discoveries are. After all, people laughed at Christopher Columbus when he said the world was round.

Perhaps we shouldn't be too surprised that we go in circles as the document says. After all most things do.

To remove the fear of death from the world will be a veritable 'trump card' against the growing unhappiness that we have today. The BACKLOG TRAUMA, if understood, can shed light on things that have previously been a mystery. For instance, when young people go back into detention over and over again, and when things are looking good for them, will inexplicably do something adverse and not be able to explain it. I know of a little girl who had experienced a very unhappy home. After two days of perfect happiness with her new foster mother[1] she was being put to bed when she suddenly said, "I HATE YOU YOU'RE HORRIBLE."

Her new mother replied sympathetically,

"DO YOU DARLING, NEVER MIND,
I LOVE YOU ANYWAY."

---

[1] The Foster Mother had looked after other children. It is possible that she had got used to the pattern of behaviour.

You see her misery had stopped charging so there was a little left in her battery and so she went into REVERSE, poor little love, but COMPASSION soon dispelled it.

Now that the backlog and its effects are being explained UNDERSTANDING WILL DAWN like BRIGADOON DID FROM THE MIST.

It is often days before it dawns on me that I am being talked to. I did improve a bit as time went on but I am still much slower than my brother would have been, I am sure that it must have originally been meant for him, but I'M NOT COMPLAINING.

I have a super friend NATHAN who acted in our shows. He has a severe health problem but has such perfect faith in God and trusts him so completely that he is able to stay his fabulous self and not let misery attack him as it would if he tried to handle it alone.

In personality NAT is so like RON it is astonishing.

If I close my eyes when he is speaking, its as though it is RON himself, so NAT is as dear to me as a younger brother would be.

He comes to the auction sometimes. I began to notice that when I saw him I would shortly see a lorry with the full name on its side of our little baby brother who died before I was born. Its not surprising that our name should be on the traders lorry as both Christian and surname are quite common, but began to notice the timing and to realise that when it passed, NAT was going to be around.

He had given me a photo album – with pictures of our shows, and had been responsible for the tape recording of PANTOMANIA. (The tape that fell into the dog's bowl). I'd stuck the album on the piano along with the tape where I could see it, sure that it had some meaning. On the cover was a picture of a GOLDEN SKY.

One day later I was very unhappy; I had given the BRIGADOON STORY to a lot of my friends to read so it had stopped their fears. This reaction thing that people can have after reading it is harmless and over in no time, but a lot of my darling friends read it at the same time. It takes longer to burn out when a lot of people get to know at once. I had accidentally worded it tactlessly too, so they were absolutely innocent and I knew that I only had to wait.

This is all applying to a few years ago. There is a logical explanation for why the 'backlog trauma' will not be so severe now, but in the beginning of this experience all was unavoidable. Until it went away I just had to be brave and wait for them to come back to me.

I was very lonely for a time so I popped out for a bit of jumbling to try to get rid of the misery I was in danger of generating and was like a grief and aching in my heart. A book fell open with a picture of NOAH's ARK with a RAINBOW REFLECTING ON THE WATER which triggered off the song.

♪ YOU'VE GOT TO ACCENTUATE THE POSITIVE ♪

I was certainly being my own 'JONAH' with the way I was feeling, as the more one concentrates on the negative the worse it gets.

In the afternoon I went off again to another jumble, trying to shake it off. I found a lovely picture of a CARGO JET PLANE, the airline was the same as CLIFF's and I think could be the type he flew, and a little RESCUE HELICOPTER for one of our grandchildren.

When I got home I recalled that 'CAROUSEL' the musical was advertised on the television for that day and thought that if I switched on, it would take my mind off the unhappiness. The play had just got to the point where the daughter of BILLY BIGALOW was being left out by her friends and was very lonely and unable to handle it.

BILLY, a bit of a ne'er-do-well had got into bad company and died tragically before she was born, but was able to see her and know what a pickle she was in and eventually was able to make her understand that he was there, and comfort came with the song:

 WHEN YOU WALK THROUGH A STORM
HOLD YOUR HEAD UP HIGH,
AND DON'T BE AFRAID OF THE DARK.

And the words go on:

AT THE END OF THE STORM, THERE'S A GOLDEN SKY,
AND A BRIGHT SILVER SONG OF A LARK.

BILLY had come to the rescue just as CLIFF had come to GLEN's and of course, the picture of NAT'S GOLDEN SKY.

When I took my old dog into the field the next morning a LARK was singing his head off and the heartache was EASED.
I must learn to do what NAT does, and just TRUST.
Just as I was writing up the notes for this story, ALEX switched on his tape recorder, and the song:

THERE'S A RAINBOW ON THE RIVER
THE SKIES ARE CLEARING
YOU'LL SOON BE HEARING A HEAVENLY SONG,
ALL THE DAY LONG.

While on my first trip to see MRS KING, (BRIGADOON STORY) in SURREY, (who's husband Jimmy was, for 'donkeys' years on the railways, and has driven the LONDON TO SCOTLAND STEAM EXPRESS), the GOLDEN WEDDING clock slowed down. We were baffled as it was always so accurate.

After my return, at the town of the OLDE TYME FAYRE, I saw one in a shop window all on its own. Underneath the words;

FORTY-TWO POUNDS
VERY ACCURATE

It struck me, that one could take that for granted at that price. Another day I noticed more golden wedding clocks, they were all over the place, the shops obsessed with them. In one shop window there were 'umpteen' ticking away except for one which had stopped. Another turned up in a box of 'odds' I had bid for at the auction, very damaged, like it had been knocked off a shelf. I still took no notice, even though the one in the window that had stopped and the damaged one were identical to JIMMY'S.

I woke up one morning with the music CORONATION SCOT, going through my head, so decided to write to MRS KING.

I mentioned the music but thought no more. A few days later there were pictures of STEAM ENGINES everywhere. So I wrote off to SURREY again, saying that I was getting STEAM TRAINS FOR

"BREAKFAST DINNER AND TEA."

I believe I had said in my previous letter how they double clues so that we can distinguish the difference between accidental coincidence.

Later in a restaurant in the ABBEY TOWN where I had seen the WELCOME BACK painting, there were double train pictures and my friend had fourteen on his wall, which must have been a recent acquisition as wild life had been his interest when I had visited him last.

I began to wonder if the GOLDEN WEDDING CLOCKS had been relevant as the trains were becoming just as numerous. Both letters were POSTED.

At the next auction there was a pile of RAILWAY MAGAZINES, (FIFTY).On the cover of the top one a picture of a steam train with a sign in the background;

KINGS CROSS

I laughed and thought, there we go again, then went off for a cup of tea.

When I returned HARRY the auctioneer was just saying "RAILWAY MAGAZINES. What am I bid? Fifty pence? Seventy-five? A pound?"

"GONE TO MRS B!"

I hadn't even opened my mouth and had been behind him. Everyone roared with laughter; they know I go for stuff for resale. What on earth was I going to do with fifty railway magazines? I had said nothing about the steam engines to anyone there, and hadn't realised their importance anyway.

When I got home, I saw the top magazine cover had a picture of the CORONATION SCOT. In the centre page <u>and</u> on the back cover?

You've guessed it? The CORONATION SCOT for 'BREAKFAST, DINNER AND TEA'.

A letter came one day to say that JEANIE, my brother's wife who lives with him in CANADA, and daughter to JIMMY was in ENGLAND. It was afternoon when I discovered it in the postbox at the gate. Earlier I had put the telly on and an advert had come on for those special commemoration postage stamps. These being TRANSPORT...

Of course, there was one of a STEAM TRAIN and it was the...

LONDON TO SCOTLAND EXPRESS

and the music accompanying?

 ♫ CORONATION SCOT ♫

Afterwards I was always tipped off when it was time to ring MRS KING. An Intercity overcoat and pictures of steam trains and references in a film to an engine driver and his ROYAL SCOT. Couldn't miss him really, they just keep going.

Twice I have done what I was told and rung her and each time she had received a letter from JEANIE.

Rail enthusiasts will notice that the stamp is of the MALLARD which was LNER and the CORONATION SCOT L M S. As I did.

I think when JIMMY was driving they were amalgamated into BRITISH RAIL. They both did the Scottish run.

A point to notice too is that the train is picking up the post.

I must have been guided into the second-hand trade so there would be opportunity to use things like the railway magazines and the shoes.

That it is all a long-term plan, thought out donkeys years ago became evident as time went on. That peoples' lives had to be organised around the multi heritage theory is extremely possible.

It is very likely that some people had to be guided to marry partners from different backgrounds so that a group of multi-heritage babies could be born before their natural evolutionary time in the hopes that one of them would be developed enough to pick up the code. (Which is what it is). Someone way back could see how much the world was going to need this information a generation earlier than if it had been left to evolve naturally.

My father, son of a ROMANY GYPSY and a SCOTTISH girl, was of a poor family, living in the Dock area of London before the First World War. He joined one of the earlier youth clubs where a famous musician VAN BEINE, offered a years' tuition on the cello to one boy if he could be found with the talent.

My father won it and was so talented that VAN BEINE kept up his training for four years and he became very accomplished; his standard good enough for the QUEENS HALL Orchestra.

My mother worked in a well-known fashion store in London as an embroideress and was very musical as well as an artist of the first degree.

She was engaged to a young man from her own world but one night he was taken ill with appendicitis and the doctor was unable to get there in time. To get over it she joined a cycling club, when she met the singing, playing, half-gypsy.

I don't know how true it is but I did hear that VAN BEINE was playing the intermetzo from 'CAVALIERA RUSTICANA' and at the point where the music fades away he faded too and gently died. That <u>he</u> could be behind some of the events that touched my father's family is highly possible.

Family stories were told of narrow escapes I can recall. A typical example was when my brother, in nineteen thirty-nine, having set his heart on flying, was accidentally given the wrong date for his examination and missed the opportunity to go into the ROYAL AIRFORCE. Probably there wouldn't have been enough pilots in the Dimension experienced enough in Spitfires and such to watch him, so it was safer to organise him into the NAVY where he was on 'B' deck when the bomb hit 'A' deck.[2]

---

[2] The explanation for why I got the code before RON and hints of how they kept him safe came to light later.

To try to write it all down now would be such a pity as there isn't enough room in this book to do RON's story justice. Perhaps a sequel can be written one day, we shall have to see.

There must have been others of course, we wouldn't have been the only ones who were kept an eye on.

Similar things must have been happening elsewhere. The daughter from an ancestral SWEDISH family fell in love with an entertaining personality. Not surprising that her public school son was happier in the theatre than on the flight deck of his aeroplane.

And the far-seeing mother of our dancing NANCY, although recognising the talent in her little girl had no inclinations towards this herself.

Not only NANCY, but her brother ADAM, was tarred with the 'multi-heritage brush'.

Working in a bank, ADAM was unaware of his potential. If he had spent even a small amount of his time creating the laughter script material that he was so capable of, I don't think he would have suffered from the illness that rendered him partially paralysed. Getting this lifestyle to suit our heredity is going to be of the highest importance in the future as we are going to have brothers and sisters with totally different mental needs. What is going to be happiness to one can mean boredom to another.

A child can feel quite guilty if he (or she) is not enjoying the same things as the rest of the family.

When I realised that my own gypsy background makes it difficult for me to stay at home for more than a few days, I bought a motorbike and 'hit off' happily to the auctions. Headaches that had tormented me for years just went away. After all, wild birds don't do well in cages and vice versa.

ADAM became ill and so depressed he was crying out with loneliness. We could do nothing for him except pray.

One day he went to ring the SAMARITANS; an organisation that we can phone to save us from suicide. He accidentally rang the wrong number. The lady who answered was in a wheelchair so he talked to her instead.

One day NANCY heard from him to say that he had found such happiness, such a wonderful friend. She had chased all his misery away, the change in him was miraculous. Too late to save him though, shortly after he died.

I have no doubt that ADAM is behind some of these ideas – in fact it would be impossible to mistake his style sometimes. Of course, he has a lady in a wheelchair to keep an eye on too, what a lot of work they <u>all</u> have to do?

One thing that is clear; these are people full of love and are teaching us, IN NO UNCERTAIN TERMS ITS POWER.

When I buy a box of odds, they all have to be restored to a saleable standard.

I had a little LANTERN two or three inches high filled with liqueur. Sent it to the shop to be sold but it was returned as it is illegal to sell alcohol without a licence.

At Christmas I was feeling very sad. It was two months since my lovely friends had read the BRIGADOON STORY and I was hoping desperately that they would come round soon. I longed to tell them of the wonderful events that they had all been part of.

The LANTERN caught my eye and was reminded of JOSH, (LITTLE DOG STORY remember?) and the time his SADIE and daughter ELLA took part in the panto 'DICK WHITTINGTON'.

We used, from the musical 'PERCHANCE TO DREAM', the song;

♫ HIGHWAYMAN LOVE. ♫

They both looked so beautiful, dressed in long flowing cloaks, and held LANTERNS that glowed prettily against the midnight blue of the night sky. As they were singing JOSH touched my hand for a moment. It said it all really. He was so proud of them.

I was tempted to write to SADIE but hesitated and know now that this was best.

As time went by, although it was Mothers Day, and JOSH's birthday, I didn't associate it at all at first when my daughter-in-law turned up with, what usually is, my regular box of Black Magic chocs, instead she was holding a gorgeous orchid packed in a LANTERN like holder.

Later I wondered, perhaps JOSH thought it was okay now to write to SADIE and ELLA, but was afraid I could cause distress, so I resisted the temptation.

When ELLA was selling POPPIES for the armistice fund I happened to remark that my father was hurt in the First World War, and I am always reminded of him when I see them.

Ever since then, the colour RED has been associated with DAD.

It hadn't been long before, that I had told someone about the PANSIE bed he had grown when I was a little girl and we referred to those tiny pansies that grow wild.

When I opened the Mothers Day card it was a picture, embroidered in my mother's style of PANSIES and I have a book entitled 'POPPIES AND PANSIES'.

It looked as if the Pansies and embroidery were saying that my parents were supporting JOSH.

I resisted for hours but later on in the evening my face started to burn and heart rate quicken so I knew that I was being given guidance.

I wrote a little note saying,

"REMIND ME TO TELL YOU ABOUT A RAINBOW AND SOME STEAM ENGINES."

It was a little while before I saw her again, but one day there she was. She gave me such a happy wave – how radiant she looked all backlog gone. I do believe a little dog yapped his way into her consciousness long ago.

I later learned that the name of those tiny pansies is

HEARTSEASE.

It is amazing how slow I've been in understanding all this. Sometimes it is days before I catch on to what is being said.

In a baker's shop I bought a cream cake and promptly dropped it on the floor. Went to buy another one, only to find that I hadn't quite enough money, so wandering into a department store contemplating a tiny packet of sweets when this song went through my head:

♪

THERE'LL NEVER BE ANOTHER YOU. ♪

Shortly after, I bought some of those little boxes of cheese. At the cash desk the young lady put them in a bag and tied it up in double knots so that I couldn't get them out again without a struggle.

Someone is trying to make me watch my health. The odd cream cake isn't going to hurt, unfortunately I could see off 'umpteen', (perhaps that is exaggerating a bit). Of course there will be thousands of people around like me in the future, but I may be the only one at present who has got as much as this together. (So I thought at the time, but have learned since, happily, that others <u>are</u> noticing unusual things).

Apart from the BRIGADOON STORY, I had kept few records and suddenly thought, if I should get onto the wrong side of the 'gauze', all the efforts of a group of very clever people would be wasted, as goodness knows how long it may take to attract someone else's attention. The world is in need of this knowledge now, so I bought a pad and pen and settled down in a café to get it on paper.

I ordered a meal and chose a helping of trifle. When it came it had no cream on. It was one of those with blobs of cream all round at intervals and it happened to be my lot to get the portion that was creamless. When I told the waitress, usually so kind and lovely, she told me in no uncertain terms that 'there wasn't any'. I do so enjoy food and felt a tiny bit peeved, but I've learned since that the Dimension people don't leave us unhappy for long.

Soon after, someone invited me to go with them to see the the musical...

'BLESS THE BRIDE'.

And after all, I do get rainbows.

As I write ALEX is talking to someone about how some people have

'A FINGER IN EVERY PIE'.

This sort of thing is happening to others.

Met a lady who had lost her son. He was only about thirty-two and engaged to be married. She couldn't handle it at all and became ill, a major operation was necessary.

When she was due to go home the following day, a church representative told her "HE CAN SEE YOU".

She found this so comforting that it must have stopped her fears. That night she ran a temperature and had to stay in for a couple of days more. (All figures).

Since then she has been able to come to terms with her loss as well as one could.

The first time I met her was at a jumble sale when she told me about her son. In amongst the bits and pieces was a MUSIC BOX. Someone knocked it and it started to play. I didn't register the tune, wished I had afterwards.

Over a cup of tea she told me how the girl he had loved met someone else. On her wedding day a MUSIC BOX that was one of the presents started to play, seemingly on its own. The music, the theme from the film, 'LOVE STORY', was a favourite tune of her son's. And the bride said...

"IT'S HIS WAY OF LETTING ME KNOW THAT HE WANTS ME TO BE HAPPY."

They get someone to knock things as JIMMY must have done with the GOLDEN WEDDING CLOCK, and can judge to a second how long its going to take for a tape recording to fall into the DOG'S BOWL. Their senses are more acute than ours, must be for my mother to see the tiny words on the picture with my brother's name (THE PICTURE FRAME STORY, as she is without her specs, and JOSH may have been telling us something by thinking up the LITTLE DOG STORY, as he used to have a hearing aid.

Soon after meeting the lady at the jumble sale, I went to another where there was a MUSIC BOX. It played the 'LOVE STORY' theme but I must always wait for something more to repeat or link in case of accidental coincidence. Be blowed if a television 'soap' episode didn't have a MUSIC BOX, and guess what it played?

That's right, the; LOVE STORY theme.

Other songs came up that were relevant, clearly saying

 'HELLO MOTHER'.

And the song entitled

 MOTHER WHAT'LL I DO NOW

There was one

'IF YOU COULD SEE WHAT I COULD SEE
WHEN I'M CLEANING WINDOWS'.

The church lady had told her "HE CAN SEE YOU." This reminded me of the remark I had made before about my mother's specs.

The code went on about windows afterwards, emphasising that they were going to 'LET THE LIGHT IN'.

When I was retyping this for the publisher, ALEX kept sneezing. He didn't seem to be able to stop until I had said "BLESS YOU."

Of course, BLESS THE BRIDE! I had forgotten to mention that half Philipino and half-English, the bride was just about as multi-heritage as can be, and had no problem with backlog when she eventually read the BRIGADOON STORY.

The reference to the specs reminded me of the time I had written "THEY'VE GOT A FINGER IN EVERY PIE.'

Days after in a café run by the same people who had made the creamless trifle (actually they make wonderful trifles, that was one special number that it was my lot to get), there were some CHERRY CAKES. On top were stuck TWO CHERRIES poked well down like TWO EYES.

Again the following week the same kind of TWO EYED CAKES but this time they had spectacles, without a word of a lie, SPECTACLES I TELL YOU!

What must have happened, when we put the cakes into too hot an oven, the top cooks too soon. When the underneath rises later it pushes up the cooked crust so the top has to split. As these had TWO cherries poked down, the crack had to GO ROUND THEM.

On a tee-shirt later I saw the words:

'HERE'S LOOKING AT YOU BABE'.

As the waitress passed me in the café, (the same one who served the trifle) quietly singing to herself, she rested two luscious cream desserts on my table for a minute,

 AS TIME GOES BY.

The little song that is associated with HUMPHREY BOGART in the famous film where he says;
"HERE'S LOOKING AT YOU KID."

But the DPs[3] had a special reason for us to say it slightly differently because they want us to get the word (as they later revealed),

'BABY'.

Alright, alright, I'll try –

---

[3] Abbreviation: DPs – Dimension People.

My son-in-law BEN lost his mum. She was a great lover of children and would spend a lot of her time looking after them. Fantastic when one realises that she had SIX of her own.

I met her two youngest girlies at my daughter's winter wedding. So pretty in their furry coats.

I remember remarking how alike they were and were they twins?

LINDA and BEN work so terribly hard, and aware that they both needed a break we discussed the possibility of a holiday, but decided that it would have to wait for another year, when they would be more able to afford it.

I had a strange old mint cutter in a box; such an odd shape so decided to keep it.

When I went into the shop where I send my things to be sold, there was one exactly like it on the counter, I remarked about it but gave it no more thought.

Soon after at the auction I bid for a sewing machine. When I got it home noticed that it was exactly like my own. Different colour, but the same model.

The next day riding down the road I saw a friend and called out "HI TOM!" Within the space of a few yards further along I saw another friend with the same name, so I called out for the second time "HI TOM!" and laughed, but still suspected nothing. We _must_ make allowances for accidents and the law of averages.

Early one morning a couple of days later I was singing quietly in the kitchen (very quietly so as not to wake the neighbours).

 YOU'VE GOT TO ACCENTUATE THE POSITIVE

ALEX came down from the bedroom. "That's strange," he said. "I was just singing that song upstairs."

There is no way he could have heard me sing it as all the doors were closed, although he may have heard me at sometime or another, all the same, WHITE CLIFFS OF DOVER or SOUTH OF THE BORDER, is more in his line so he found it curious enough to mention.

The same morning I went to see my daughter LINDA and told her of the coincidences and made her understand that she must realise how important this material is and that if anything should happen to me she would find it in my music stool. I said that BELLE, her mother-in-law, had been close all the time.

I left her to go shopping when later in the supermarket who should I meet but LINDA and her little son, beaming faces both. Immediately I had left her house she had picked up a letter from the mat. One of those that we sometimes just throw away (English people will know what I mean) in it a FREE HOLIDAY).

On returning home I spotted a book called 'THE IRISH TWINS' on the side.

Next evening, (and it had been a chilly day) met NANCY. We'd seen each other briefly at that afternoon's jumble sale – she said,

"YOU BOUGHT THAT FURRY COAT I SAW THEN, LOOKS NICE."

I explained that I had had it for sometime but asked "was it identical to mine?"

She replied, "OH YES EXACTLY, LIKE TWINS."

NANCY told me once when she and CLIFF were in the theatre, in the middle of her dance act he and his partner led a DONKEY up the aisle. They had to carry on dancing in true professional manner.

I suggested that we ought to treat all DONKEYS with suspicion.

Off to the auction soon after, TWINS all morning; TWIN BOOKS, TWIN COAL SCUTTLES, TWIN SHOES, TWIN MOTOR BIKES, TWIN PIXIES in a picture, and HARRY...

"WHAT AM I BID? GARDEN ORNAMENTS TWIN DONKEYS!"

I had said in my letter to Mrs King (CORONATION SCOT STORY)

"WATCH OUT WHEN THINGS DOUBLE."

By this time it was summer. On the train on the way to the seaside a little girl started to sing...

 JINGLE BELLS JINGLE BELLS
JINGLE ALL THE WAY.

Our little boy took up the challenge with...

 LITTLE DONKEY LITTLE DONKEY ON THE DUSTY
ROAD
GOT TO KEEP ON PLODDING FORWARD
WITH YOUR PRECIOUS LOAD

As everyone knows, this is a CHRISTMAS CAROL that tells the story of the road to BETHLEHEM, and the little DONKEY'S part in taking MARY there with her unborn baby JESUS.

After that, they always saw to it that this little 'DONKEY' (me) had a 'CARROT' to keep her going.

The Friday after meeting LINDA I bought some pork chops, when I went to put them away they were missing. I couldn't find them anywhere. At a fete the next day I had forgotten that the fridge was empty. The previous day I hadn't taken enough money while shopping so I was doubly short of food for the weekend, having lost the chops. Without intending

I bought two beefburgers from a stall, and won, in a raffle, a bottle of wine.

There were hundreds of CREAM CAKES too, all lined up on the counter in the village hall. I was even allowed to eat one. Mind you, mine was a bit scanty with the cream.

On my return found the empty fridge and the close shave I'd had. (We had no freezer then). Without the beefburgers we wouldn't have had anything for Sunday's dinner.

I was keeping notes about the coincidences by then and had recorded that I had met LINDA at the MEAT COUNTER and afterwards remembered it was the CREAM CAKE COUNTER, and realised that it is most important to get details right when, that Monday morning ALEX went to put on his wellington boots and 'lo and behold', there inside were my CHOPS! They must have been knocked off the work counter and fallen into them and so were useless, needless to say.

"SLOWDOWN, NEGATIVE MEAT COUNTER.

BE CAREFUL, MUST GET DETAILS ACCURATE CON."

I think they are referring to my exaggeration with the cream cakes and why they included the wedding clock that fell off the shelf and the one in the shop being ACCURATE to link.

I think too that ALEX's auntie (PEGASUS STORY) and BELLE could have been with me that day we found the chops. Just before this story I had found a book, along with a copy of 'THE WINGED HORSE', called 'DON'T LEAVE YOUR WELLIES IN THE HOUSE'. On the back were EIGHT CHILDREN IN A ROW. Auntie had talked of how uncle's wellies never came into the house. Needless to say I should have taken her advice. On the other hand I expect she's quite pleased that I didn't as they use my mistakes to their advantage.

LINDA and BEN were unable to take the holiday. Meanwhile I was sure that the Dimension People would think of something. One day I went over there to find that they had gone away together for a few days.

The current record was playing the song:

 ISN'T IT ROMANTIC

And their holiday destination? Of course,

PARIS. Where else...

As time went on I found that I was only picking up a fraction of the clues. Sometimes it has been months before I have put some of them together but as with everything, it becomes easier with practice.

That reminds me, I must remember to get LINDA's birthday card, as it is the day before

VALENTINE'S DAY.

In time BEN'S business began to pick up, so he and LINDA were able to afford a Mediterranean cruise. He said that they would visit CASABLANCA, the scene of the romantic film with HUMPHREY BOGART and INGRID BERGMAN. When BEN told us, he quoted the line,

"PLAY IT AGAIN SAM," as people sometimes do.

Just before, in a programme featuring LAUREN BACALL, who was married to HUMPHREY, (very happily I believe), she said that he never said "PLAY IT AGAIN SAM," so we've got to be careful.

Shortly after BEN'S remark what should I spy in a charity shop but the video of the film (now why aren't we surprised?)

It is true that HUMPHREY doesn't say "PLAY IT AGAIN SAM," but Ingrid, his love in the story, does say...

"PLAY IT ONCE SAM, FOR OLD TIMES SAKE
PLAY IT SAM, PLAY AS TIME GOES BY."

This way they teach us the importance of ACCURACY.

The television linking with songs and records became hilarious. A typical one...

Mr brother was always concerned that I didn't study other languages. His efforts to teach me French were totally in vain. He made a recording of himself and JEANIE, singing a song about some FRENCH GENDARMES who were not as bright in their jobs as they should be. It goes...

 WE ARE BOLD GENDARMES

We have two friends who used to write the funny scripts for our shows. Both went into the Dimension within a short time of each other. The name of one was CHARLES STREET. Anyway, there was this funny telly series about the FRENCH RESISTANCE called 'ALLO ALLO'.

As I was writing to my brother one day I remembered the GENDARME who speaks in a funny language, like BISSES instead of BUSSES and THONK instead of THINK, and it struck me suddenly, that the words were MY TYPING MISTAKES.

I hit the wrong keys all the time, and I had written GIT instead of GOT! (When it comes to typing I <u>am</u> as 'thick as two short planks'). I thought, "BUT THERE'S ONLY ONE GENDARME in the programme," and as you will notice too, that things have to link or repeat.

The following Friday I turned the telly on and straight away a reference was being made to the programme that NANCY had appeared in.

The day after we were both in the supermarket. I had bought some fancy TEA BAGS for ALEX when she said "I FEEL DROWSY, JUST AS IF I HAD TAKEN TRANQUILLISERS."

She had been working hard on her little cottage and needed a good nights sleep.

She was also beginning to realise that GLEN was going to be alright, so the tiredness would have been made worse by backlog burning out.

The next week was the 'ALLO ALLO' programme again and SOME MORE GENDARMES HAD BEEN PARACHUTED IN.

A little lady NANCY'S size drank some drugged TEA and then STOOD ON HER HEAD. NANCY had stood on her hands chatting away merrily whilst upside down too, in the programme she had appeared in.

Then I remembered I had asked CHARLIE STREET to write a parody on that GENDARME song. He had been unable to do it because he went into the Dimension before he could.

And the message...?

"THE CODE WILL BE UP RONS STREET?'

You can imagine what must have happened, the Dimension people laughed like Billy-o when my words came out so funny on the typewriter. I think they said "HEY, WE CAN USE THAT," when inspiring us to write as they must be doing.

One day after struggling all afternoon to try to tidy up my terrible typewriting, I turned on the telly to relax when who should be on there but the latest offering produced by the same writer as 'ALLO ALLO'.

'OH MR BEECHING'.

This is another funny series about an old railway station and the steam trains.

The station master is just about to translate ETHEL'S TYPING MISTAKES. And very funny they were too.

I think they were reassuring me about the bad typewriting, which does seem to be unalterable, and worrying makes it worse.

In the early days of our shows I was quite obsessive about including anything even remotely saucy. The word KNICKERS was most definitely OUT. One day I changed the script and made them say "KNICKER<u>BOCKERS</u> IN A TWIST", instead of KNICKERS!

AND THE DIMENSION PEOPLE HAVE NEVER LET ME FORGET IT!

Along with TWO DONKEY ornaments that had been standing on the telly one afternoon, had been a local NEWS programme item. A lady was being interviewed with a mug of TEA in her hand. The camera inexplicably honed down on it a couple of times.

It may have caught other people's attention as it was, on the surface, an odd thing to do as the mug had little relevance to the story it seemed to me.

The code became more decipherable with practise.

Shortly after I rang NANCY from the phone box, as we were not on the phone then, and said,

"BEEN HAVING DONKEYS AND MUGS ALL DAY – YOU ALL RIGHT NANCE?"

She answered that she had been trying to get a message up to me all day to say that she had an invite to go to an evening jumble sale in someone's car and would I like a lift?

When I returned from the evening out I put the telly on and there was this funny programme. An old lady was just about to conduct a séance and was just saying...

"IS THERE ANYBODY THERE?"

The rest was so saucy I haven't got the nerve to repeat it, but NO SHADOW OF A DOUBT, I thought, ADAM of course.

The film would have been made before he went into the Dimension, but there was no doubt in my mind who had been responsible in influencing someone to choose that episode.

Next day when we saw her, NANCY said...

"CON, DID YOU SEE LAST NIGHTS EPISODE OF A...?" She said the old lady was exactly like her mother (who is with ADAM) "PULLING UP HER DRAWERS, JUST LIKE NANA USED TO DO."

As she was watching the programme and realising it, the phone rang. It was her grandaughter to say...

"QUICK, PUT THE TELLY ON, THERES AN OLD GIRL ON THERE JUST LIKE NANA, PULLING UP HER DRAWERS JUST LIKE SHE USED TO DO."

Then I remembered I had asked CHARLIE to write a sketch using BOY SCOUTS.

It was so kind of MR DAVID CROFT to give us permission to use this dialogue. MR JEREMY LLOYD shared the writing and we have them both to thank for so many wonderful programmes over the years, like ARE YOU BEING SERVED, along with MR JIMMY PERRY (DAD'S ARMY) and MR RICHARD SPENDLOVE (OH, DR BEECHING) and other hilarious ones. DAVID produced and directed most of them.

Do writers and producers of these comedy programmes have any idea of the extent of their wonderful effect on the fate of the world? To raise people's JOY level is the most useful thing that can contribute to saving the whole lot.

It may be important to mention here, that only one or two remarks are relevant, all the rest of the script writing will be the writer's own.

They certainly did make the most of these programmes though.

MR CROFTS AUTOBIOGRAPHY is now on sale in leading bookshops and what a wonderful read it is, but then what else can we expect. Oh! I've forgotten to include the title; it's YOU HAVE BEEN WATCHING...and is published by BBC BOOKS.

I got better at it but it became impossible to record all the code films and plays, not to mention the announcer's remarks and the advertisements.

Another nice one was when they used that wartime resistance programme again, 'ALLO ALLO'.

In the afternoon I had been 'tipped off' that DOCTORS and RED CROSS NURSES were to be the 'in thing' for that day and to be 'BE PREPARED'. (Here come the BOY SCOUTS).

Recording it I had written RED CRISS NESSES instead of RED CROSS NURSES. Anyone who has seen 'ALLO ALLO' will know what I mean about the Gendarmes funny language.

In the programme there were these two chaps disguised as NURSES. One holding a bed pan, in it was a secret radio. They were in danger of being discovered talking into it by a superior who asked them what they were doing.

So one said of his (her) companion, to get them out of it, "SHE'S A MEDIUM, HER FRIEND DIED WHILE SHE WAS SITTING ON IT," and the other one said, into the bed pan,

"IS THERE ANYONE THERE?"

Later we learnt that CLIFF'S partner, who he had worked on stage with, is a guest artist in one of the programmes that I suspect he has influenced. So his fear that a show business career would be uncertain was unfounded and had he stayed where he belonged he may well too have been successful.

GLEN is a natural comic too, positively brilliant at making people laugh as well as so many other attributes. It was afterwards that I remembered saying to a doctor friend of the depressing negative telly programmes,

"WHAT WE NEED IS A RESISTANCE MOVEMENT."

Just after I had spent a bit of time on this page, in a 'soap' episode on the telly, a dialogue went, on the part of an airline pilot;

"IT'S JUST A GLORIFIED BUS DRIVER."

Wouldn't be conclusive on its own though.

One day when I was writing CLIFF'S story an old friend came in. Proper old country character he is. Lives over the hill with his geese and goats and gets around in wellies and overall. Actually he is a retired FLIGHT ENGINEER FOR AN AIRLINE and he said in his broad Devon accent,

"OI USED TO BE BORED STIFF SITTING FOR HOURS JUST LISTENING TO THE ENGINES."

Travelling in a bus one day and wondering if I should include this in the book. Immediately around the corner came a RED WHITE AND BLUE coach with the same name as his AIRLINE.

They use RED WHITE AND BLUE for the word POSITIVE in the code.

This reminds me of a song that CLIFF used

I GET NO KICK IN A PLANE
FLYING TOO HIGH WITH SOME GUY IN THE SKY
IS MY IDEA OF NOTHING TO DO...
That's from the song I GET A KICK OUT OF YOU

In my records there is a lovely story about the WELLINGTON BOMBER that CLIFF flew in the war, but there is no room to include it here. In the new episode of the funny resistance programme, they capture a WELLINGTON BOMBER and go on about WELLINGTON BOOTS as CLIFF has done before.

Looking back now I am sure that they were reminding me of accuracy with the boots but in those early days I wasn't so proficient as now, at picking it up. The BBC is running repeats of these episodes so I may be able to see where I may have missed some of the code.

OH DEAR, what is the world coming to. Its going to be taken over by POPPIES AND PINK KNICKERS.

I had written PINK KNOCKERS by mistake!

One day ALEX came in with two short planks of wood! What a nerve they've got! (ADAM, very suspect). We might just as well get used to it, they aren't going to go away. Not while we need their ideas anyway, but then what else can we expect? With funny script writers and people who are determined to

MAKE LAUGHTER TRIUMPH.

My father was shell-shocked in the First World War, so it is he who rushes to me with COMPASSION when my nerves go to pieces. (USED TO GO TO PIECES).

I found this out in the dentists one day.

I'm not usually worried about going, the modern technology is so fast and painless now and one gets used to it. But when having a 'misery battery charge' about something (and I was experiencing the 'backlog' from having my fears stopped by the BRIGADOON TRIP). We become more prone to things that would not normally worry us. This day I was positively scared stiff although aware that my apprehension was illogical. I kept saying to myself I've been to the dentist for forty years without worrying before, didn't think it showed though.

Passing a young man on his way out, he said sympathetically,

"RELAX, RELAX."

Just as the dentist was poised with his drill, had a feeling of irrational panic. The music that was playing started;

 OH MY BELOVED FATHER

And all distress vanished.

Looking back now I can see what must have happened.

When we have a high degree of unhappiness, or suffering from backlog trauma it is harder for the Dimension people to make us hear them. I think they have to have a lot of DP's at once to see us through at times like that.

They use the song...

SHOULDER TO SHOULDER

They know that my teeth had to have attention and that the backlog would not be burned out before the appointment. When we can't hear the subconscious voice they think of external ways to comfort us, as on the day of the SEAGULLS when LUKE came along at the right time. (He hadn't read the BRIGADOON STORY so wasn't hampered by the 'backlog' as others had been).

When the music came on and the dentist crew who turned it on at the right moment may not have had any misery level, and so were easier to direct, as they are a happy lot. I was suddenly aware of DAD'S SYMPATHY, neutralising misery. The music must have raised my JOY level which would make it easier for them.

It was ages after, before I remembered that the young man who said "RELAX, RELAX" was holding a little girl, probably his own. DAD uses the soliloquy from CAROUSEL and the words,

♫   MY LITTLE GIRL.   ♫

when he wants to comfort me. (I was a little girl when he had to leave us).

One Sunday morning couldn't get on with anything and feeling pressured on the verge of generating misery charge as I needed a change of scene.

Must seem amazing when one thinks of all the miles I do each week.

Theres the ABBEY TOWN, the LITTLE TOWN – where the shop is where I take stuff for resale, the BIG MARKET TOWN where the auction is, and the BOOK TOWN – where I take books to sell and where I had singing lessons.

You wouldn't think I would need a change of scene with all that popping around would you? But I have inherited the genes of my gypsy grandfather and the need to be moving on is always present. It was some time since my trip to SCOTLAND, so all the signs were coming up.

I took the old dog for a walk but was conscious of the fact that I <u>must</u> keep at this and had so much else to do and getting 'strung up' about it.

Just down the road a little boy ran up to me with a POPPY in his hand, and said...

"HERES A FLOWER FOR YOU CON.

RELAX." ... I did.

Things were cropping up RED all over the place one morning. DAD around, I thought. At the auction, noticing a box of odds that would do for resale. Later returned just in time to bid from the back to find that I had got the wrong box. Instead of china I found MUSIC. All the old favourites, including POET AND PEASANT with which my father used to make the piano rock. Some pieces I used to struggle with too but most of them were his. I used to be lazy about learning the Italian symbols and in one book were implicit instructions, written by hand. I had thrown it onto a chair where it fell open at BRAHMS' HUNGARIAN DANCE Number TEN, but I thought it was number FIVE that he used to rattle off like Billy-o. It was some time after, before I noticed that the cover was RED.

The next morning I was sitting in a chair with the electric light on, when I could see the reflection of a RED lampshade in my mother's picture, I laughed as I sang the 'jumpy' bit from ♪ POET AND PEASANT ♪ The RED light seemed to dance about too. I've had that lampshade for ages but its reflection has never caught my eye before.

I KNOW, I was sitting in a different chair and it was on the opposite side of the room to where I usually sit. ALRIGHT, ALRIGHT, I <u>will</u> get down to some music again one day.

As I write a knock at the door.

Someone asking if I can sing for a charity evening.

My brother has a most beautiful smile; the resemblance to the film star TYRONE POWER is positively uncanny.

Just after my quandary about the music, a film came on with him playing the piano in his naval uniform, the lovely smile flashing towards the camera, as RON'S does in a photo we have of him.

And the piece was suspiciously like one of the HUNGARIAN RHAPSODIES that my father used to play (I think it was LITZ No 7). As soon as I had written it down a film came on and the dialogue went, while someone is looking at old photos...

"THEIR SMILES DON'T CHANGE DO THEY?"

I didn't get down to checking a recording of LITZ'S No 7 for several days after this. By then I was a little afraid that I may not have remembered the tune correctly, as we had no video then and accuracy is vital. Immediately I had typed this a film entitled 'ANCHORS AWEIGH' with EIGHTEEN GRAND PIANOS! SEVENTEEN played by young people and children. The music most definitely

A HUNGARIAN RHAPSODY

At this point I disturbed something with the typewriting ribbon and the words came out in RED lettering. I know
I know, RELAX

I think my father is saying that any HUNGARIAN DANCE or RHAPSODY should be associated with him.

After this, wearing a RED shirt and a RED SCARF to match, I set off for the auction happily singing the song

 PLAY GYPSY PLAY

I bid for some music and the auctioneer said,

"GONE TO THE LADY IN RED," and repeated the same words with the next lot I bid for.

On leaving I heard a shout from a friend "where did you get that scarf? I need one just like it for my musical act." I said, "What's the song?" He replied

"PLAY GYPSY PLAY."

When the book was complete I was satisfied with the continuity and comfortable about its length but it was so untidy. I never really learned to type properly so I was faced with the prospect of making it look less disreputable. The very thought alarmed me dreadfully and I couldn't see how on earth I would be able to improve it, as I make the same mistakes all over again when retyping.

I was sitting, trying not to panic, when ALEX turned his radio on. The Brahms HUNGARIAN DANCE no FIVE was playing (in the RED covered book).Of course it was lovely but the music had changed to GYPSY LOVE and PLAY GYPSY PLAY before I began to connect it. Then it was followed up with the INTERMETZO from CAVALIERA RUSTICANA, so soothing. Even then I hadn't really 'caught on', would you believe it? until the announcer said

"RELAX..." with (and then he named the radio station).

I made alterations that improved it quite a bit and went to put it away. From out of the envelope fell...

A BRIGHT RED RIBBON!

I must have put it in there to mark a place at some time. At the same moment a kind neighbour interrupted me with a gift of POPPY SEED CRISP BREAD.

Oh dear, who on earth is going to believe me? Sooner or later EVERYONE I think.

As time went by I realised that I was never going to completely master the typing so I toyed with the idea that I could find someone who could help me; but back then the book content would have been too traumatic for just anyone to be able to type.

I hit on the idea to try and find someone who was already aware of the Dimension people, so I contacted the local Psychic Society, who so kindly found someone who is half-Polish and half-English and had no problem with backlog trauma.

Thank you, thank you, dear lovely girl for all your time and skill, which you gave lovingly with no thought of reward.

Like the proverbial BLUE BIRD, you flew in one day and saved me.

If anyone has never suffered from the distress of a panic attack some of the following chapter will be meaningless, but if one is unfortunate enough to have experienced this – and acrophobia could come into the same category, then the following narrative could be invaluable.

Its a pity I have had to abbreviate so much but all the same its surprising how much we can learn from a little tuition.

While out on the bike one day, having been on the road for about half an hour, I suddenly felt a dreadful attack of insecurity and depression. I know now that the cause was only 'backlog' having been at home for some time which for me always generates negative charge. As soon as my journey is well away the misery that is generated if I can't get out, STOPS and so the negative charge has to burn out.

Alarmed, I shouted HELP! Before I knew what had happened I had taken a wrong turning and had to go a long way round to get back to my usual route. Of course, the change of scene helped to quicken up recovery because seeing different places raises my JOY level. Its gone in a short time, especially now that I understand that 'backlog burn out' is all it is. At one time I used to catch the next bus home not realising that the feeling of exhaustion was perfectly normal and most of all TEMPORARY.

We can see how important it is for us to get the hang of this, as it is the key to so many situations that could be relieved by us understanding it.

I noticed as time passed that the bigger the misery level the longer the gap before it manifested itself. When I have had to stay at home for a long period in the past, the backlog has not come on until the day after. On the day of the motorbike the horrid feeling came on half an hour after I had left the house having only been stuck at home for days. If it had been weeks it might not have come on until the next day or even the day after that.

Although understanding that there is generally a gap before the backlog unpleasantness attacks us. I do know of a friend who experiences it before she leaves the house after being confined, so there may be individual differences according to the strength of our misery. And we must bear in mind that we can recharge the battery with the distress caused by the backlog and get another dose later. This is much milder though and more likely to be non-existent if we fully understand it, because although it is very uncomfortable we don't get alarmed.

The form our backlog takes will vary with different people. If we have been worrying about something and then the anxiety is relieved.

It wouldn't be difficult to work out what our tendencies are and once we understand the backlog principal, our comfort is that it is TEMPORARY and will burn out, henceforth we will not recharge it with worry. Its not surprising that this has not been generally understood before, although I think doctors are on to it. I believe the term they use is POST TRAUMATIC STRESS DISORDER. Of course, with such things people may need a medical check, but even though they feel so awful it is highly possible that nothing will be wrong.

At the beginning of this experience, I found that excitement caused indigestion pain. Aniseed and charcoal from the health food shop soon worked in my case, for the over-activity that so much JOY can cause. Our doctor would advise us about this. He may have to resort to some himself 'bless him,' when this new understanding of the Dimension people comes.

Sometimes, when retiring after years and years of work, it can be a little while before the JOY and freedom can be fully appreciated, or a young mother who may have had a difficult confinement cannot understand why she seems to have no happiness in the baby. Often, she is not able to tell anyone. This can be severe and must be the worst one for recharging the battery with guilt. Sometimes the answer to distressing problems can be shatteringly simple. It disappears quickly once we understand what is happening to us and normal feelings return when the misery charge has burned out.

Shortly after I had written this, in a television interview a young mother described a feeling of BEREAVEMENT after she had given birth to her baby, which backed up the 'opposite way round' theory, or fact rather.

There could even be a link with overweight. If we have been seriously overweight for many years it can be a subconscious worry. It's a well-known fact that after dieting successfully for a little while the very moment we realise that the diet is working, an overwhelming need to eat something wrong and spoil the whole thing is very common, because our misery has STOPPED.

Once we understand that this reversal is normal and will be only TEMPORARY, the negative will burn out and the ability will return to master the problem and will not recharge once we understand it.

It has been known for the gap between a worry stopping, to be much longer before the negative comes on. The important thing is to understand our own personal tendencies. The more we do, the quicker it will be to overcome the problem.

I can judge almost to the nearest hour how long a 'backlog' will take to manifest itself so whenever I've been worrying about anything for a time and the worry has resolved, I leave the bike at home and catch a bus until its all gone as I may not drive as well. I have a raised blood pressure too at times like these for about an hour, sometimes even less. It returns to normal – the pattern always the same, so I don't recharge it with fear.

Of course, the time will come when we don't have really serious misery levels but for the moment we can get ourselves through quite efficiently until that day arrives.

On the first day I sent the original notes to the publisher, after returning home from the post office, I turned the telly on and a film was about to start entitled...

TWO YEARS BEFORE THE MAST

My mother used to talk of it and was a favourite of hers. As most people know it is a story of a struggle to get a book published. I was relieved to see that after some effort they were successful and it closed with a SHIP IN FULL SAIL gliding confidently into the future. Just after this, an advert: for a film with CARY GRANT called SINGAPORE LADY. I had sent a copy of the manuscript to my brother in Canada. He spent a long period in SINGAPORE while in the NAVY, that was before returning to England to serve as an instructor at the same naval school where, as a boy, he had helped man SAILING SHIPS, climbed a CEREMONIAL MAST and later was stationed in an old country house where he, (of the scientific mind), wrote home to tell us of GHOSTS!

My training in noticing the Dimension code had to be a gradual process though, as I am only able to assimilate a little at a time, not being very quick to pick things up easily. Its all an apprenticeship like in TWO YEARS BEFORE THE MAST.

After I had typed this, put the telly on for a break; POPEYE and a SHIP IN FULL SAIL about to say...

"YER SAILS WANT TRIMMIN A BIT."

They don't want me to be carried away?

So dutifully cut some out and thinking, will have to watch out for confirmation that I've got it right, never having written a book before, so could they think of some way to direct me?

In the garden, I noticed lots of CONVULVULUS – a climbing plant which grows wild but is very pretty. As I had not been in the garden for ages it was even climbing around ALEX's radio aerial. I saw the sweet peas were stuck with it too, so got some scissors and had to cut the things away. Such a shame as they were so pretty but were choking the flowers.

The stories all have so many clues that can't be recorded. To try to write them all down would overcrowd them, so I've been told, by way of a book entitled SIMPLE PRUNING to be careful not to overload the lot.

They have since hastened to say "THEY AREN'T COMPLAINING." So I must have got it right.

Have a dear friend ANNA, known her since we were teenagers. Divorced many years before, hadn't seen 'AL' since, although her boys go over to see him sometimes.

Her son's wedding day due, all great joy except for the meeting again after so long, hung over her head like the 'sword of Damocles'. Off she went to the BOOK TOWN to get a wedding present, feeling her happiness could be dulled by how she would handle it.

She arrived a bit too early to catch the bus back so had to wait in the bus station café – and who do you think had decided to have a cup of tea? You've guessed it? There AL was as large as life, so together they waited for the bus. What a lovely natter they had, all embarrassment gone, and what a smashing wedding it was…

My brother was due to visit me from CANADA with his devoted and beautiful JEANIE. As right as ninepence they are. He knew immediately when he met her and in his own words "I'VE FOUND HER, THIS IS IT," and it was.

The Sunday before his visit a film on Canada, Niagara Falls – the road I had travelled along with him on the way to the Falls many years ago; the hotel where he took me to a banquet, and the places where JEANIE and I went. In fact a right old memory lane. The musical ROSE MARIE as well which everyone knows is about the CANADIAN MOUNTIES. RON, like NAT, can be very funny. He had signed his first letter to us after he had gone to live in Canada when leaving the Royal Navy;

'RON OF THE MOUNTIES'.

I used to be reminded of my mother when I saw the little flower SPEEDWELL and have remarked that it reminds me of her blue eyes. I found a Christmas magazine with ideas for a little theatre and a pantomime picture of FAIRY SPEEDWELL and underneath were the words 'ON WITH THE SHOW'; meaning this book. A couple of days later, before RON came to stay, when preparing the dinner I found a little weed in the spinach and had, for some reason, put it in a little vase on the kitchen windowsill.

When he arrived I noted the tired lines around his eyes and knew that the news posted to him about the coincidences had made him a bit shattered.

That evening I knew of the strain he was trying to hide, JEANIE too, being the daughter of the engine driver behind the 'CORONATION SCOT' story. The reaction was normal and not serious but it must have been a shock to realise that JIMMY can still influence stories of a steam train.

Just before they came, ANNA had said as she caught sight of my mothers picture, "IT COMFORTS ME…"

As we were going to bed, both of them noticed the picture and stood looking at it in silence, I remembered ANNA's remark about the comfort and I think they felt it too.

At dinner the waitress turned out to be a lovely friend who had been the first to read the BRIGADOON STORY. I was relieved to see that she was very much recovered and we had extra helpings of every thing.

When the time came for us to say goodbye we were standing in front of the picture. Quite suddenly the lines left RON'S face, as it dawned on him that the poor boys who went down with HMS BARHAM, didn't stay in the cold sea after all, and the fear that he will one day have to be parted from his beloved JEANIE was gone. I held him close, realising that the backlog, like a candle, was all burned out. Clutching the pile of railway magazines, and with the Tyrone Power smile restored, he said goodbye.

Immediately after they had gone I glanced at the piano. RON and JEANIE had been playing, and had left propped up, a piece of music; a selection from PERCHANCE TO DREAM. In it was a song my mother uses when I need comfort,

     WE'LL GATHER LILACS

This is a musical that tells the story of a couple who came back in different lifetimes to meet too late, but they find each other in the end. When Ivor Novello wrote the music to that story he must have been inspired by the people in the Dimension. Lying on the floor was a tiny card with a design of LILACS. JEANIE must have dropped it while looking at photos. It was from my own wedding and lovingly written on it 'FROM ANNA'.

I went to prepare dinner when I noticed the little weed in the vase, it had formed a perfect little SPEEDWELL. Turning the tape recorder on, the song came up...

♪ I DREAM OF JEANIE WITH THE LIGHT BROWN HAIR ♪

I recalled that she had changed her hair colour. The pretty light brown shade was the first thing I saw when she came in.

I had bid for an old BANJO for NAT to restore. 'Be blowed' if RON hadn't said, "JEANIE bought me a BANJO for my birthday." Of course everyone knows that the composer who wrote JEANIE WITH THE LIGHT BROWN HAIR was Stephen Foster who also wrote minstrel songs like A BANJO ON MY KNEE, so when these came up on the radio or on records I look out for news of RON and JEANIE.

Soon after ALEX came in playing his own tape recorder. The theme from LOVE STORY. I said not recognising it straight away...

"THAT'S NICE WHAT IS IT?"

He replied, blissfully unaware of what he had been part of,

"SOMETHING TO DO WITH A RAINBOW."

And the document goes…

2000 YEARS AGO A STABLE AND A STAR WERE CHOSEN FOR THE GREAT PRODUCERS STAGE, BUT THIS TIME THE VISION OF MUSICIANS AND WRITERS OF FAIRYTALES AND SONGS AND DANCES WITH WHICH HE CHOSE TO WORK, SO AS TO BE ABLE TO TELL US THAT LIFE IS SUPPOSED TO BE A FAIRYTALE, WHERE WE MEET OUR RIGHT PERSON AND WHEN THIS SECTION OF LIFE IS FINISHED WE WAIT FOR HIM OR HER, AND THEN OFF WE GO AGAIN WITH THE KNOWLEDGE, THAT IF WE LIVE WITH CHRIST'S PRINCIPLES WE WILL ALWAYS BE IN THE RIGHT PLACE AT THE RIGHT TIME…

ALEX came home with another more reliable motor bike. The great day dawned when I was able to ride around the coast for a holiday. It's logical that spending so much time making costumes and scenery that before I found the auctions I couldn't earn money. Although ALEX is generous and kind, my budget wouldn't stand any luxury.

A few minutes before I left, ANNA came in holding a five pound note and insisted I take it for some little treat.

On my arrival, it was ten minutes past five. I rushed up to the town and booked a seat for the theatre. There was only one left, the cost FOUR FIFTY, and the show?

PERHANCE TO DREAM

Sometime ago in my early motorcycling days I was given an old flying suit. It must have been used in the thirties or even earlier. Wore it until it fell to pieces and it's only lately that I have realised that it must have been a collectors item.

When 'flying' around on the bike I had often thought that when I write to RON I must sign, 'love from AMY JOHNSON'. I don't think I ever did though, so that could have been one that misfired on the DP's part. Not long after this I came across a book entitled 'THEY FLEW ALONE'. This told the stories of pioneers in long distance flight. Among them the story of AMY JOHNSON, who was the first woman to fly solo across the world. In it a photo of AMY wearing an identical suit to the one I was given.

As time went on, I realised that the Dimension people wanted me to keep quiet about this book. It costs a tremendous amount of money to send it around to publishers, (by our standards anyway), but, was unable to ask my family for help. There is no way they would have allowed me to be short of money if they had known.

ALEX does know that I am writing but I have learned even with him to keep it a low profile for the moment, and so, like AMY, I will have to be prepared to 'FLY ALONE' for the time being.

While sitting with this page before me, my son 'breezed' in with an offer to pay for a theatre trip for ALEX and myself and then 'breezed out' again with the remark...

"CAN'T STOP, THIS IS ONLY A FLYING VISIT."

When the bike eventually packed up, LINDA and BOB turned up with a BRIGHT RED new one.

Oh dear, they will have to know the whole story one day, I KNOW, I KNOW, 'RELAX'...

At one Saturday jumble sale I picked up a leaflet about an archaeological site and at the same time a book illustrated by the WILDLIFE artist who stayed with us when I was a child. My cousin's wife SHEILA has written a lovely book on CONSERVATION with the same title as the leaflet, so I embarked on my first attempt at fortune telling by expecting a letter from her.

It didn't come until the following Wednesday, but the postmark was the day before I found the leaflet, as it was second class. The date inside the letter was three days before, so it must have been left on the side, giving someone in the Dimension time to look for something to get into the jumble sale, or what is possible they already knew about the leaflet and book and so organised the letter accordingly.

Just as I was writing down the incident, ALEX came in playing a recording of a conversation with SHEILA and TONY. So that's how some fortune telling is done.

A little while after, I tore from a book a picture of a KINGFISHER and left it on the mantelpiece to frame. A letter came from SHEILA to say that she and TONY were coming on a visit. It was written on a 'RNSC' CONSERVATION TRUST card. The picture on the front;

A KINGFISHER.

Underneath it were the words from a poem which referred to a rainbow.

It would be the first time I had seen them since I had sent the BRIGADOON STORY, so I was a little apprehensive as when it is read we sometimes can't always be our normal cheery selves for a little while.

Our little grandsons were with us at the time, so before my cousin's arrival I decided to take them out to see a pony in the lane, where I had been given the POPPY by the little boy.

Earlier that day ALEX had brought in some POPPY SEED HEADS and left them on the table where our little boy must have seen them.

As we walked down the lane he spotted two POPPIES in the hedge and said...

"LOOK NANNY, DON'T YOU THINK WE OUGHT TO TAKE THOSE POPPIES HOME TO GRANDPA?"

DAD saying 'RELAX', so I stopped worrying...

We had a lovely visit – but then my cousin TONY and SHEILA too, could be multi-heritage after all.

I later found the whole poem about the KINGFISHER in a book by ARTHUR MEE and was reminded of the ARTHUR MEE quite valuable books I came across when very hard up once. At the same time I found one by CHARLES DICKENS; THE LIFE OF OUR LORD. I put it on my pillow, intending to take it downstairs and had forgotten to. On going to bed it was still there so I opened it. On the first page was pictured a little girl kneeling by her bed saying her prayers. Overhead an angel-like, or motherly figure, watching over her and in the corner the name of the illustrator; MEE.

There's no doubt they listen to our conversations and remember things long after we have forgotten them, and there is a possibility that a lot of little incidents are a lead up to something spectacular. Occasionally though their plans misfire. An example was when I found one afternoon that I had picked up three books entitled...

JUST THE VERY THING, LONDON BUSES and A GUIDE TO LONDON.

The bus book and the guide were very old. With the BUSES I was delighted to see a picture of the store in LONDON where my mother did her training. It was taken before her time, the name clear above the window. On another page, a photo in which the name of the store was masked by the bus, but taken at the same time as my mother had worked there. I was curious to know if the dresses in the window could have been some my mother had had a hand in, (she used to design the embroidery to go on them). The sign on the bus was LADBROOKE GROVE, so I thought I could work out which way it was facing; a clue into whether or not the shop was hers as in the other picture. She used to talk of the busses often and say that she had to tip her hat sideways to get in as the 'tifters' of those days belonged to a more roomy world, and of course I had THE GUIDE TO LONDON. TIFTERS? Cockney rhyming slang for HAT.

The next day I saw a pile of books on LONDON, they were very old so thought they would make a good price and made no attempt to get them. They were a perfect set. The bidding went up to ONE POUND and I stood there and let them go.

There is an explanation though; just before the booksale I realised that my darling friends were over their backlogs and back to their wonderful selves again, so my own misery stopped and of course then had backlog to burn out too from the relief of worrying about them all – which took the guise of feeling exhausted for a short time – so was not able to respond to the Dimension 'tip off' to buy the books.

If people can be sympathetic when we're in the backlog state – which I know is sometimes not easy as we can be quite disagreeable and our own worst enemy, it will disappear more rapidly. Which just goes to show

THE POWER OF COMPASSION.

Jill used the expression WE'RE NOT IN THE DRIVING SEAT again. The next day I didn't have enough money to go to my usual auction but found, amazingly, a few old clothes I didn't know I had. I take antique clothes to the BOOK TOWN so had no choice but to go that way instead.

In the street I was handed a leaflet entitled,

'THE INCOMPARABLE CHRIST'.

In it a reference to my mother's picture,

'BEHOLD I STAND AT THE DOOR AND KNOCK,
IF ANY MAN HEARS MY VOICE AND OPENS THE
DOOR,
I WILL COME TO HIM.'

Of course I thought it could be an accident, but if it was meant for me then the trouble which must have been gone to must indicate its importance. The DP's work, as a team so someone will have had to find a publisher of religious texts and get them to chose those words.

They set up the books and when it failed they reminded me of the antique clothes so that I would still have to make the journey that way, being short of money for the other auction. I wondered if my mother was pointing out that I hadn't given her picture the right title but it is unlikely, as she is aware of the importance of getting on with this and would not want me to waste time, so I was puzzled.

There I met ALEX'S nephew. Hadn't seen him for years, accompanied by his talented little boy who had just passed his music exam. Written across his tee-shirt was the name of the band in which he was playing. In the post office I scooped up some bits of paper, having written something at the desk, to leave it tidy. When I got home found it was an advertisement for –

MUSICAL INSTRUMENTS, afterwards remembering, that everywhere I had gone that day, people had held the door for me, in the stores and the post office.

Then the penny dropped! It was the town where I had been given VOICE training.

"IF ANY MAN HEAR MY VOICE AND OPEN THE DOOR
I WILL COME TO HIM."

I recalled shortly before, it had been the BOOK TOWN where a young man had come out of a shop with the name STOKES across his overall and someone left a plastic bag with STOKES written on it in the seat next to mine. In a café and on the pavement a sign advertising STOKES...

GOSH! Something marvellous! Why haven't I thought of it before? Everyone knows about the famous medium DORIS STOKES who appeared on Australian television and Canadian radio. She would have conversations with the people in the Dimension and has written five books all with VOICES in the title.

She was often able to prove to the world that she was genuine and wouldn't have been invited a second time if she hadn't been. DORIS used to be able to see them too, although I wonder if they were able to suggest to her "I'M WEARING A

BLUE DRESS" and kind of paint a picture in her mind, sort of thing. What a good job they made of it too. All the same the conversations were real as the Dimension people were able to identify themselves to their loved ones.

In her books DORIS talks of her father and how he liked auctions. I learned later that he was of ROMANY descent. That the fortune tellers (and I mean the accurate ones(were MULTI-HERITAGE has been noticed before, so what is giving me absolute JOY is WE ARE ALL SUPPOSED TO BE LIKE DORIS. That the normal thing is for everyone to be able to hear their loved ones in the Dimension.

The class distinctions and our tendency to only marry our own kind meant that the intelligence got held up in its evolution and it couldn't develop fully and DORIS and people like her have a more complete mind. As we all know ROMANY GYPSYS shared our ways to only marry their own kind too, but being taken prisoners by the Lords of Romania, when it was likely that half-class and half-peasant babies would have been born, they must have had a head start. By the time they had travelled through so many different countries the exception to the rule must have occurred and the more developed mind evolved. No wonder they could tell fortunes as they must have been 'tipped off' by the Dimension people whose intelligence far outweighs ours.

The travelling in time theory that some books speak of could, I think, have evolved out of the fact that the Dimension people can store memory and can calculate how the future can develop. I must be careful when writing about time travel as it is only my personal opinion that they just have twenty-four hours in their day like we do. There are many books on this subject and they may well be accurate. The main thing with this one is for us to understand the effect of the backlog trauma.

The group of Dimension people who are organising this book may wish to cover other aspects with a sequel, or even leave it to other writers. In time we shall see. In my own case I have only been able to hear single words or phrases but always they are relevant to the code guidance.

I must have the mind of the future for them to guide me into writing JOSH's message about the little dog. It was accompanied by a racing metabolism and although it did no harm they had to think of a way to guide me without the physical discomfort. It is obvious that my mind is not so evolved as DORIS'S, but WHO'S COMPLAINING?

The clues carry on so much that it would take too long to record them all but I am convinced that I have got it right about DORIS and am happy to see that her books are in great demand. Among them are VOICES IN MY EAR, and INNOCENT VOICES IN MY EAR. That one is about children. She says that sometimes at night she has to, sort of, 'switch them off' as they are so anxious to make us understand that they are there, that lots would try to talk at once. What a lot we owe to people like her who OPENED THE DOOR TO THE OTHER DIMENSION.

All the evening after the BOOK TOWN, telly programmes were jogging my memory of her. I should have 'twigged' my father wanted me to think of DORIS and MUSIC. In one programme there were about THIRTY-FIVE CHILDREN, ALL PLAYING CELLOS!

All those PIANOS! all those STEAM TRAINS! All those GOLDEN WEDDING CLOCKS! We've got to hand it to them,

THEY'RE TRYERS.

Just as I had written that, ALEX was playing a recording of a melody (blissfully unaware of what I was writing)

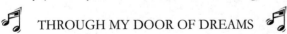 THROUGH MY DOOR OF DREAMS

Shortly after a television programme came up entitled, HAVE I BEEN HERE BEFORE? This was an experiment where several celebrities underwent a kind of regression into their past lives. It was astonishing how many facts they were able to find to back up the past life theory.

As the people taking part seemed to relive short periods of time I must keep an open mind.

Their experience <u>could</u> be a form of TIME TRAVEL.

A drop of
golden
sunlight

Not far away from the ABBEY TOWN is a huge hill. I found it by accident one day before my trip to Scotland. All around were the most glorious views. No matter how far I looked I could see no sign of pollution or anything that could mar its beauty. It was that day I knew we must be eternal and everything that lives now is permanent in some way, but I had no idea how it could be, only absolute certainty that it was so. I parked the bike and happily burst into song...

♫   THE SOUND OF MUSIC.   ♫

Halfway to the ABBEY TOWN one day, stretching across the sky were black clouds, behind them the most spectacular SILVER LINING. I have never seen anything like it except in those old paintings with a religious theme so I stopped the bike to look. Cars came by and to my surprise carried on regardless; puzzling, as the rays were extraordinarily beautiful. I felt shaken as there seemed no logical explanation, so I thought, perhaps my theory that all could be explained was incorrect.

As the days went on more information came in – to record it all would take too much space, but the explanation was simple. There were three jumble sales at different times. TWO O'CLOCK, TWO THIRTY and THREE O'CLOCK, a few miles in between each. One in a village to the left of me, one to the right and one at the ABBEY TOWN on the road that I was on.

I didn't decide which jumble I was going to until ONE O'CLOCK.

The Dimension people can WEATHER FORECAST. They knew that autumn was going to provide us with some interesting cloud formation and that it was going to stretch across a wide area that day, so they influenced people to organise jumble sales in that direction. They were safe with three then waited until ONE O'CLOCK, before making me chose the one that was going to be in the most spectacular place. They probably had to wait to see themselves where it was going to turn up the best, so of course the amazing display was just over the road I had chosen. Behind me there was only blue sky and of course no jumbles in that direction. They went on to explain that the reason why the other vehicles didn't stop was because THEY CAN MAKE ME SEE SUNRAYS MORE VIVIDLY THAN OTHERS, and sort of, sharpen my perspective.

A couple of days later I met the postman with the returned manuscript. Feeling sad went off on the bike and as I was riding along I could see the huge ABBEY TOWN HILL where I had sung THE SOUND OF MUSIC. Right over it was another SILVER LINING, spectacular and beautiful, directly over where I had found such JOY. When I got home, ALEX was playing his music...

 LOOK FOR THE SILVER LINING

It was the ABBEY TOWN where I saw the painting of the STEAM TRAIN and the pictures in the café. It strikes me that JIMMY is very fond of the ABBEY TOWN.

I needed stuff urgently for the shop as I was afraid the teeth or bike may need attention again. You would think I would have more faith by now wouldn't you?

On my way to a village jumble sale, its opening, TWO-THIRTY, I came to a railway bridge. There were lots of people with cameras 'happy as crickets' who said that the famous steam train, THE FLYING SCOTSMAN, was due to leave the ABBEY TOWN at TWO-FIFTEEN. And was reminded of the WELCOME BACK painting at the OLDE TYME FAYRE. I sadly carried on my way, as I was afraid to be late arriving at the hall with ten minutes to spare, so if I had just had trust in the Dimension guidance I still could have seen the train.

In an advertisement paper it said the FLYING SCOTSMAN was coming again the following week, so I planned a jumble in the ABBEY TOWN. I set off in plenty of time to look for a vantage spot but when I got there I couldn't find the hall where the jumble sale was to be held. Now I go through that town every week, but for the life of me I couldn't recall where the hall was, or the railway lines. It was like the day I couldn't remember NANCY's name. When I did eventually find the hall there was no time left to look for the vantage spot as it was nearly time for the jumble sale.

Standing in the queue at exactly TWO TWENTY-FOUR – when I heard the train. It came closer and closer and became so loud, like it was just beyond the hedge. I have never been the steam addict that my brother is. (It is logical that he would be married to the daughter of an engine driver). I can fall in love with anything if I can travel in it but, as she came close she BLEW HER WHISTLE. It was so loud but such a lovely sound I wouldn't have missed it for anything. The people in the queue seemed not to notice so I was puzzled.

When riding through the ABBEY TOWN again I saw that the railway lines were quite a long way from the hall and although it seemed that they were just over the hedge they were too far away for the sound to be so clear. Even with the wind in the right direction it still would have been impossible in the normal way, for it to sound so loud.

The Dimension people hadn't meant me to be at the vantage spot, so I was deliberately made to forget the whereabouts of the hall and railway lines, so that they could teach us how they can sharpen our senses to sound and sight.

I found everything I needed at the jumble sale. It is time I learned to have confidence in THE PEOPLE IN THE DRIVING SEAT. Of course this is explaining how they are doing it. Our perspective is sharpened so that the one remark in a film or book can be made more clear than the rest, and like the colours of the rainbow too, in the kitchen and the field that day.

I was reminded by this of a piece of music that I was struggling to play in the beginning of this experience, from the musical SOUTH PACIFIC. It is called

95

YOU'VE GOT TO BE CAREFULLY TAUGHT

This song actually has a negative theme, but the Dimension group has made it clear that the negative must be reversed.

About this time THE SOUND OF MUSIC came up again with the song, as the hills were reflecting in a bus window,

 I HAVE CONFIDENCE IN ME (MEE)
It is definitely time I did.

One day later on in the year, I had the unfortunate experience of having TWO fears stopped in one day. (No room here for all the details). I had found a copy of ARTHUR MEES, ENGLAND series and as it was near Christmas the proceeds would help towards the expenses that had worried me. I rode home singing happily, completely forgetting about backlog reactions.

I sat down to study the telly programmes to see that THE SOUND OF MUSIC was scheduled for the next day. Suddenly my mind started to flit strangely with odd things, I thought light headed? So I said to myself 'stay calm and the DP's will tell me what is wrong'. Could it be overtiredness? I put some music on and a HUNGARIAN RHAPSODY was playing, so I thought, DAD please help me. It was more severe than ever before, like the horrid feeling we can have when at a great height. I forced down some food as hunger can make us have some odd reactions too.

A knock came at the door, it was a young girl. She wanted to make a Christmas decoration because she didn't have anything to do and did I have a LOG? I said, "We'll have a look round the BACK to see what we can find," and I was so grateful for the diversion. She picked up a BRUSH-HEAD before finding the right shaped one, then took TWO LOGS. I came back indoors when she had gone, then it dawned. No wonder!

I'd had TWO worries brought to an end that day ITS BACKLOG! DOUBLE BACKLOG! And the BRUSH-HEAD? My grandmother who is in the Dimension uses the song from the musical SALAD DAYS,

GET YOURSELF SOMETHING TO DO DEAR and the words of a song so comforting DON'T SAY GOODBYE FROM THE SHOW,

 WILD VIOLETS

Well we don't have to say goodbye, do we?

So I stopped worrying and prepared to wait until it went away. I got out the hoover and gave the floor a good old clean. By the time it was done the horrid thing was nearly gone. It returned slightly the next morning, having recharged the 'battery' the previous day a tiny bit with alarm, but it was soon over.

I thought, I shall now get organised to watch THE SOUND OF MUSIC and look forward to the lovely rendering of,

 I HAVE CONFIDENCE IN ME. (MEE)

From then on the colour VIOLET was always associated with my grandmother.

BILL POWELL transisted; can't call it dying anymore. ALEX told me at five-thirty one Monday evening. I used to know ROSE, BILL'S wife, years ago and engaged to her brother VICTOR was almost one of her wonderful family. When VICTOR and I broke off our engagement we still stayed in touch for a little while.

In those days though, without transport we couldn't get to see our friends, even when they may only be a few miles away. When I did become mobile, years had passed and the gap seemed too wide somehow and I didn't like to just turn up.

On the morning after ALEX told me, I had this longing to be with her, but I was in a terrible quandary whether or not to go and pay a visit. One is always afraid of making things worse. I decided to tidy up a box of hair curlers; very out of character as that morning or any morning for that matter, tidying up was not my first consideration. I came across a POWDER COMPACT. Inside it was the brand name which was ROSE'S full Christian and surname before she was married and when I knew her. It repeated underneath and I bore in mind that to distinguish things from accidents they have to repeat or link in some way. On the lid was a tiny basket of flowers.

Not long before my mother left us and during the time I was with VIC, who is in the Dimension now, she embroidered a basket of flowers and framed it. Not having done any embroidery for years I was surprised when she suddenly did that. It was incomplete too, so I didn't care for it. She wasn't interested enough, having done so much in the past and taken it for granted like NANCY did with her dancing. Normally my mother could make flowers live. The little basket of flowers on the compact lid didn't have the overlapping edge either so I decided to chance it and go over to see ROSE.

When she opened the door she was so glad to see me. It was as though it was only yesterday that I had seen her last. On the wall there was a picture of A JOCKEY WITH HIS CAP TURNED BACK! I couldn't keep my eyes off it. After learned that BILL had painted it himself. I told her of my experiences but she was not as surprised as some, as she, as a teenager had known strange things of her own, and I believe ROSE and BILL have more than a bit of multi-heritage.

A couple of days later in a local television news programme was an artist in the act of painting a picture of... A JOCKEY WITH HIS CAP TURNED BACK!

It was amazing how like the one on BILL'S wall it was.

The Sunday after a film came up starring CARY GRANT. BILL was so like him to look at, one expects CARY to sing the SEPTEMBER song or say "BY JINGO" just as he used to do. I gave ROSE all the notes on the manuscript to read and worried for days in case she should go into the backlog trauma.

The expression 'THINK PINK' kept coming up in magazines and telly and the happy day dawned when I had a letter to say that she loved the notes, and was sorry when they ended.

On my next visit I left her just before a shower of rain. On one side of the road a RAINBOW started to form; in a field opposite the other end had begun too. I stopped, cars going past, and slowly the centre filled in to form a complete bow. Like my friendship with ROSE, the RAINBOW closed up and became as though it had never been separated. A little aircraft began circling as though it was going through it, like a tiny silver bird glinting in the sun.

When I got home and picking greens in the garden, another two little planes began circling exactly over my head, in the sunshine the SPEEDWELLS were shining up at me. The song currently playing in the kitchen...

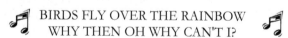

BIRDS FLY OVER THE RAINBOW
WHY THEN OH WHY CAN'T I?

One day when I was in a hurry, I grabbed a jersey I had bought at a jumble the day before. In the mirror I saw reflected on the shoulder a BIG PINK ROSE. I caught sight of a gardening paper, on the cover advertised a BLUE ROSE and inside, another. The only time I have seen BLUE ROSES was when a friend said, "they turn back to PINK after a time." I expect horticulturists have overcome this problem now as that was sometime ago.

Propped up on the piano was the song…

♩ RED ROSES FOR A BLUE LADY ♩♩

The PINK ROSE on my jersey was reversed in the MIRROR while ALEX burst into song with that tune too; I thought, could ROSE be BLUE? The expression THINK PINK kept coming up on the telly and advertisements so I wondered, perhaps it was time to visit her.

I found ROSE very sad as she missed her dear BILL dreadfully. She said, "It looks as if this is only meant for you Con, as I haven't had a 'dicky bird'."

Not a sign had she been given, and very disappointed she was too.

We know now that her high misery level would have affected her ability to pick up the code but I was able to cheer her a little, and we ended up rolling around with laughter at some of the Dimension antics.

We recalled that day that BILL had driven us to PORTLAND BILL LIGHTHOUSE and she got out photos. In one, BILL is holding a MUG, in another he is IN THE DRIVING SEAT OF HIS CAR. ROSE had felt the impulse to snap him while they were driving along.

In my next box of 'odds' there was a LITTLE BROWN JUG. On it the words PORTLAND BILL. Little jugs started to do the 'breakfast, dinner and tea' stunt that by now I was getting familiar with, nearly always BROWN ones and LITTLE ones.

And the song goes…

 HA HA HA YOU AND ME
LITTLE BROWN JUG…

One day the auctioneer said…

"WHAT AM I BID FOR A BIG BROWN JUG?"

I thought, that's curious, surely the Dimension group could always count on HARRY to get things right?

Following this, ROSE was showing me lovely china that BILL had given her, among it an old antique JUG.

I turned it upside down to see the maker's mark which was P B. P B is BILL'S initials REVERSED, hence the BIG BROWN JUG (opposite way round). And the song goes…

 I DO LOVE THEE…

Shortly after a film and the last words before the end CARY GRANT says to the girl who was his wife in real life…

"I HAPPEN TO LOVE YOU VERY MUCH MRS ROSE."

The film is full of courage and compassion and is based on a story called,

ROOM FOR ONE MORE.

The first anniversary of my trip to Scotland came along. Two days before the date of 'BRIGADOON DAY' a film of the place where I had met all the people from different parts of the world, and the next day there was a reference to the musical BRIGADOON. It was the day BEFORE though, I was wondering why all the linking things were happening before.

In the morning after the films I had to see the dentist. I had no worries about it, it was simply that my teeth had to be seen to. He couldn't fit me in during the morning; unusual as he is so accommodating in an emergency. I understood and went home to return in the afternoon.

It had been raining. On my way there was a detour; I had to go a long way round to approach the town by a different way. This must have altered my timing a bit. It is unusual to go that way and at that time of day.

As I went over the bridge GOSH! I couldn't believe my eyes, THERE WAS A RAINBOW ON THE RIVER! And THAT WAS BRIGADOON DAY.

Every year the anniversary was observed unfailingly. One year when I was listening to a recording of a Christian song, I looked up to see that the picture on the wall of JESUS knocking at the door was bathed in an oblong of GOLDEN LIGHT. The shaft of sunlight through the window exactly framing the picture. The Dimension people must have noticed that the patch of light falls on the wall at sunrise in October. The BRIGADOON TRIP was the second week in that month. ALEX must have been made to hang the picture in the right place. I made a mental note to photograph it when it happened again, but double glazing was put into our home and to my dismay found the light was altered with the new window shape.

As time went by a new tree grew in the garden. The sunlight began to shine through its swaying branches causing the GOLDEN LIGHT to flicker on the picture, seeming to give the figure life and movement. The effect was as glorious as the original.

I think the whole colourful plan was thought out around weather conditions, as they must be able to forecast them roughly months ahead. I found in a box of 'odds' a dictionary of films. All had been watched by a team of people who make criticisms of the standard. Our DP group must influence the programme editors which to chose, or what could be even more likely; they influenced the films when they were being made, then organised events to coincide with them.

For example, an advertisement for ALLBRAN, where a little boy says, "CONCENTRATED? WHAT'S CONCENTRATED?" At the same time they see that I am eating ALL BRAN.

'CONCENTRATE CON.'

Then that will be followed by a film or play and the people in the film will be wearing a HAT similar to the one I've seen in the jumble sale that day and then another film will come up soon after, REPEATING the HAT. Another example, I got a 1930's CLOCK, and that same afternoon saw one exactly like it in a film. This became more frequent now they do them every day. Of course they probably <u>have</u> been doing so all along, but it took two years for me to get even remotely proficient in deciphering the code.

As time went on, there were more stories concerning BILL and ROSE. BILL uses racing and many have sequels but there's no room to include them here.

Whenever it was time to go over to see ROSE, as well as PINK THINGS and ROSES, they use those ARUM LILLIES. So I duly did what I was asked just after the BRIGADOON ANNIVERSARY, and went over to see her. I told her about the 'RAINBOW ON THE RIVER' and she produced a painting by BILL of the same BRIDGE!

About this time I found, in another box, MUSIC, together with a song book. In it the titles;

LAVENDER BLUE and FOREVER AND EVER.

Once I sang the first to VICTOR and he sang FOREVER AND EVER to my strumming on an old piano.

When on a shopping trip, I ran into an old friend who used to live in a little tucked away village where I had worked in the big house as a maid. VIC and ROSE lived there too. URSULA had to go to work, so after a hurried word we said goodbye.

Months later I took another trip there. Just as I was walking down the street and singing quietly to myself...

 LAVENDER BLUE DILLY DILLY.
LAVENDER GREEN...

There she was walking towards me. This time I was invited to her home for coffee. I was amazed at how much we had in common and surprised that I hadn't got to know her more when we lived in the tucked away village. VIC used to talk of her and say "she makes me laugh," meaning that she was such fun to be with, his affection brotherly. She never met anyone that she liked enough to marry. When it was time to leave she gave me some flowers.

I still had a little vase on the kitchen windowsill. All through the summer it was never empty; as soon as the flowers faded someone gave me more.

One morning I was wondering what would happen in the winter and would they stop coming? When I noticed the flowers my friend had given me were like SEA LAVENDER. (It grows on the Norfolk coast where I lived, long ago and far away, as a child). They dry and become EVERLASTING (Statice). I went out straight away in a different direction than usual, parked the bike, unaware until I returned, that it was directly opposite a shop door, over it the name...

DILLYS.

The next morning I settled down to write to ROSE and tell her of the LAVENDER BLUE, when I overheard ALEX say, as he was showing his brother photos,

"THAT'S VIC WITH SING."

"WHO'S SING?"

ALEX replied, "VIC'S DAD IS NAMED SING."

VIC was stationed in SINGAPORE when in the Army and his dad used to often talk about SINGAPORE and FAR AWAY PLACES, and 'SING' was a nickname. Immediately afterwards the telly went on about a tourist place that I had visited with him, the only time I ever went there. The same place came up again a few days later for the second time. On the piano was propped up a copy of the song that VIC used to sing; 'FAR AWAY PLACES.'

On the same evening of the photographs, ALEX called

"COME IN HERE AND LISTEN TO THIS."

The radio was playing VIC'S song and in my mind I could hear his 'Bing' like rendering of,

 FAR AWAY PLACES

I leave it to you to guess what he was telling us. The document goes, ONE SPECIAL PERSON WHO WE WAIT FOR... and real love like the LAVENDER BLUE FLOWERS lasts,

FOREVER AND EVER.

URSULA's name came up repeatedly afterwards, sure enough just after I had finished writing this someone called her name in a film. They must be working out exactly how long it is going to take me to write the stories so it looks as though I must be up to schedule.

I had been worrying that I was slow getting the book done, so anticipated staying up half the night although dreadfully tired, but have had my attention drawn to a film that CARY GRANT made, as well as SINGAPORE LADY, (the name of a plane).I had wondered where it came in though, as it seemed to have no significance, but I've 'got it' now, it is entitled,

'WALK DON'T RUN'.

After the LAVENDER BLUE story LAVENDER BAGS kept turning up. I'm snowed up with them now – haven't got the heart to get rid of any of them. We'll have to have an extension put on the house at the rate they are coming in.

After I had written that, a little girl came up to me at a jumble sale and said...

"HERE'S A LAVENDER BAG FOR YOU."

Early in the 1950's THE MOON WENT BLUE! VIC used to meet me in the evening from work at the big house. One night he exclaimed,

"LOOK, THE MOON IS BLUE!"

It came up on the radio the next day with the explanation that it was caused by dust from Canadian forest fires.

VIC uses the song BLUE MOON and look...

a BLUE ROSE

A gardening advertisement and the following telly ad along with others.

(Film the Moon is Blue (1976, U)
Innuendo laden comedy romance
With William Holden ** 96587865

See what they mean about not overcrowding the book as they keep it up continually?

At the market I bought FAGGOTS. These are a traditional dish popular in the south of England and are delicious. I hadn't eaten any for at least two years. They were a bit too salty so I told the stall owner who was glad I had pointed it out to him, these being his first batch of a new venture.

When I got home I noticed the kitchen was full of salt pots, pepper pots too, all over the place. Umpteen 'out of one box' and others that had been accumulating for weeks. That same evening ALEX came home with FAGGOTS. I should have suspected, but didn't especially, when I had bought a big white pot; on it the word in huge letters, SALT. As I was examining it for the shop found the underneath rim was chipped, although perfectly usable not suitable for resale and surely I had seen it somewhere before? IT WAS MY OWN. I had given it to a friend and she must have passed it on to the Scouts' jumble sale. I found I had bought my own sugar bowl too.

The evening after the FAGGOTS a knock came on the door and there was an old friend I hadn't seen for years. Have only met BOB once since I used to stay with his mum ANNE before I was married. His face so strained and white, he had so kindly come thirty-eight miles on his motorbike to tell us that his step-dad had transited into the Dimension. PAUL used to live 'along of us' in the tucked away village. When they married he and ANNE had a little house right beside the railway lines. When the trains went by the salt and pepper pots used to vibrate.

A particularly noisy train made them SHAKE and RATTLE and she used to make FAGGOTS.

ANNE was already in the Dimension and up till then her identity hadn't come in. I was in a quandary whether or not to tell BOB about the coincidences. The trouble is that when we have just lost someone, our misery generator is going round faster than ever before. Immediately after a bereavement is not the best time to have our fears stopped.

As he and ALEX were talking, in my mind I asked the Dimension people what to do when suddenly I remembered that ANNE had a foreign-sounding name. Although she was English her attractive continental beauty must have come from other shores. Yes! She must have been multi-heritage, I thought, so decided to tell him. He said,

"WE HAD FAGGOTS FOR TEA YESTERDAY FOR THE FIRST TIME IN TWO YEARS."

I have never seen a face come back to life so fast. I put my arms around him and we were half-laughing and half-crying. Mind you the laughter won. I gave him the current record that had been playing that day. ANNE spoke with a low contralto voice. The song on the record was sung by an artist with the rich contralto tones she used to use and the words go so lovingly…

 FOLD YOUR WINGS OF LOVE AROUND ME

ANNE loved the IVOR NOVELLO songs.

I still worried for a time in case he went into the backlog trauma as its onset can be delayed for quite a while sometimes, although reassurance came in time and time again on the Dimension code. Then one day ALEX said…

"THERE'S A MESSAGE FROM BOB ON THE CB. HE SENDS HIS LOVE."

Next day I bid for what I thought was a box of china, when close, found that I was the proud owner of

THIRTY-SEVEN SALT AND PEPPER POTS!

Now just in case you think this couldn't happen to you, a little warning. A couple of weeks back within a short time of each other, different people wanted to give us

FIVE SOFAS!

Shortly after, ANNA came in and said…

"I'M GETTING A NEW SOFA CON, WONDERED IF YOU WOULD LIKE THE OLD ONE AS IT'S STILL QUITE GOOD."

There was such a puzzled expression on her face when we burst into laughter.

One cold and rainy day a market stall holder decided to pack up. He started to sing…

 "TIME TO GO HOME, TIME TO GO HOME."

The song is from a television series for children that was very popular before the programmes became so sophisticated, called ANDY PANDY. I am happy to see that this charming series has been revived after many years with other delightful characters from 'WATCH WITH MOTHER'.

The next day I set off to catch a bus to a completely new town, but before leaving I noticed a new clock that ALEX had hung on the wall with a PENDULUM. On the way, there was a street with my mother's maiden name and simultaneously a lady on the bus asked the time, afterwards, realised my attention was being sought. On arrival I spotted a little child wearing an ANDY PANDY pyjama suit in his pushchair and going into a shop. Remembering the song I followed and what should I see there but rows and rows of CLOCKS.

The first dozen had pendulums and the rest (there were eighty before losing count) were round, some with happy faces, like the one that I had painted for the kitchen scene in our production of CINDERELLA. The lot were all working at once, the entire wall was covered with them.

Up till then a dozen identities had come in. They were easy enough to recognise. Similar dodges like the steam trains and the embroidered picture applied to them all one by one. The clocks were a 'tip off' that there were more people in our Dimension group than I had realised.

A lovely friend who lives a few doors away invited me in for a chat one afternoon. I thought how cosy her room was and I enjoyed the comfort of her armchair and delightful company. As three a clock chimed. I didn't take much notice until a little while after another one chimed. I began to register when still ANOTHER joined in 'CUCKOO CUCKOO'.

This was merrily accompanied by 'CHEEP CHEEP' from a watch lying on a side table. I said "Goodness, how many clocks have you got?" And would you believe it? There was one exactly like the GOLDEN WEDDING CLOCK! Isn't it priceless? She has a beloved cat. At night she calls him home so that he can be safe and warm. His name is ANDY PANDY, (PANDY for short).

I think they are saying that in TIME we will find answers to our problems as there are now so many of them to guide us and that it is only a matter of TIME before we can all 'COME IN OUT OF THE COLD' so to speak. That may explain why they keep on about FURRY COATS too. I think they are saying that they've got us 'ALL WRAPPED UP'.

As I write I hear the strains of a song coming from the telly accompanying an advertisement for sofas...

 IT'S A WONDERFUL WORLD

OH! THE SOFAS! At the beginning of the ANDY PANDY films a posh little voice says...

"ARE YOU SITTING COMFORTABLY?"

They don't leave it there; as soon as I wrote this, up it comes again! Would you believe it?

Are you sitting comfortably sir?

Are you sitting comfortably ...?

Are you <u>really</u> sitting comfortably?

As I write ALEX is playing his music again;

♪ THERE'S NO PLACE LIKE HOME ♪

As I was checking this page ALEX received a birthday card from LINDA. It had six children in a row looking over a fence into a field. They are avidly watched by a dog just like our dear old DANNY. (BELLES STORY). BELLE was DANNY'S previous owner.

The brand name of the card was ROYLE. The DPs have been on about ROYALTY for some time. Now what are they saying I wonder?

It was about fifteen months since the rainbow in the field and THE LITTLE DOG story. The next day the identities really got going. Over a period of time they came in two by two and to my astonishment they were everyone I had known except for a few. It was explained why they wouldn't be mentioned until later. I was a bit worried about AUNT DAISY (Tony's mum). She didn't turn up with the others, then one day I noticed double daisies in JOSH'S garden, and sure enough even though it wasn't yet spring, all the field was covered with them. Hundreds, the Dimension people must have had to wait until they came out before her identity could come in. Soon came the song IN THE GOOD OLD SUMMERTIME. There was good reason for why they wanted to make the most of AUNT DAISY as they later proved.

While watching a film and catching bits of the dialogue that were relevant, I noticed too that the opening number was the same song that I had sung during our last production in which we used a NAUTICAL theme. Halfway through the dialogue goes…

"I'LL PAY FOR THE DISHES." By a waitress, having dropped a trayful.

The day before I had seen a broken vegetable dish identical to the china that I had dropped, whilst working in the big house as a maid in the tucked away village. I used to break things all the time. Of course, once I had begun to worry, the worse it became and was in danger of going through the whole lot, always saying...

"I'LL PAY FOR THE DISHES."

I never had to pay for them; the lady in the big house was so understanding about it and knew that there was some reason for the unfortunate tendency. My time with her was of the highest importance.

We had a gardener who was retired from the ROYAL NAVY. One day he left the radio on using up the battery. The lady thought I had done it. She believed me when I said I hadn't, but it remained a mystery to her as I couldn't very well 'split' on NOBBY, PETTY OFFICER CLARKE, (actually CHIEF PETTY OFFICER I mean, sorry NOBBY). By using the dialogue and linking it with events at the auction, he was able to say, "SORRY ABOUT THE RADIO." After the dialogue film, all the sailors came in. UNCLE GEORGE, ex-NAVAL MARINE used without a shadow of a doubt THE DRINKING SONG and OLD FATHER THAMES another one he used to sing. COMMANDER BOYD too. Together we had taken part in a play, HMS PINAFORE, where he had to use his own uniform. He had trouble with the sword as it swung around a bit when we danced.

At the auction a NAVAL SWORD for sale NAVAL OFFICER'S DRESS UNIFORM too. Couldn't miss him, well couldn't miss any of them really, especially when a film came on of a young man in a NAVAL OFFICER'S uniform, several times falling head first, having merrily tripped over his sword (CARRY ON ADMIRAL).

It was COMMANDER BOYD who revived my interest in Christianity, which was to play a vital role in the plans to get our attention. The Christian teaching of the POWER OF COMPASSION was essential and without it none of this would, in my own case, have come about I am sure. I do not mean that other religions are not powerful in teaching love and joy – of course they are. Collectively they must have been responsible for saving the whole lot.

Although COMMANDER BOYD was terminally ill, he coped with it so serenely that no one could know him without realising that something spectacular was keeping him going, just as NAT handles his problems so amazingly with his trust in JESUS.

Mind you, JESUS is a superstar, no wonder he is called 'THE SON OF GOD'.

As I write this the strains of a dramatic melody are coming from the living room...

♪ JESUS CHRIST SUPERSTAR ♪

When the identities came in they were too many to record. The lovely BUTCHER and BAKER who used to call at the big house both turned up. I kept seeing BATHTUBS everywhere. In a field, gardens and yards. Also, a turquoise green one; that Verdigris colour that copper goes when it is old, and a play – THREE MEN IN A BOAT. One day NANCY was out with her dogs when she found some BATH TAPS; exactly what she needed too. On the news a story of some people who were shipwrecked. The only things they had to cling to were two BATH TUBS! Wished I had taken more notice of that story – it was quite a while before I saw the connection.

I was rubbing myself down after a bath two days later when it dawned on me. The old rhyme goes...

RUB A DUB DUB, THREE MEN IN A TUB,
THE BUTCHER, THE BAKER, THE CANDLESTICK
MAKER,
ALL POPPED OUT OF A HOT POTATO.

Thinking as I was dressing, or was it a cold potato? When a huge hole appeared in my tights and my heel POPPED OUT like a BIG POTATO!

But where was THE CANDLESTICK MAKER?

Shortly after a new identity came in. Once, for a concert, I was asked to sing the song

♪ OTHER PEOPLE'S BABIES ♪

This is a song of a children's nanny.

As a young girl of fifteen I had taken a job as a nursemaid. This was when we were in the north country. The lady who I worked for and her family were so loving and kind. They had a beautiful old house and I was so happy with them. We had to come south; it was my fault that I didn't keep in touch. The last time I saw her she was wearing a big wide-brimmed hat and looked like MRS MINIVER in the famous film. I have never forgotten her; so good so fair. She gave me a little book of Dickens, A CHRISTMAS CAROL and still have it.

The day after I had written THE THREE MEN IN A TUB story, the little book turned up at the jumble sale. Exactly the same version. I bought it and thought of her straight away. The clues came in again and again. She must have remembered everything we had done after all this time. It would be fun to record it all but it would take too much space. There can be no mistakes as the law of averages couldn't produce so many linking things. In several films ladies wearing big hats and her name was in so many of the clues.

It was just after the war, we couldn't get any work done in those days as so many skilled people were in the forces. They had some copper pipes that used to make the washing green, turquoise green. Of course they would have got them fixed when workmen became available. Then those things were unavoidable. She used the COPPER pipes in her identity clues (and I've just remembered that I sang RUB A DUB DUB to her little girl). How comforting it is to think of her in my life again after so long and now I have TWO copies of A CHRISTMAS CAROL.

When I had written this story I searched for the original book, but was confronted with boxes and boxes of articles. My cupboards are full up as I have been trying to keep all the things they are using for the code and I didn't have time to find it. A couple of days later, auction Monday, I found another identical copy and have never seen one like it since.

More identities of other employers came up. As I didn't stay anywhere long I had got to know a lot of people. The babies theme kept up, like references to JELLY MOULDS. At the dinner table once I went to turn out a blancmange from one. It was perfect, couldn't have wished for a better shape except that it landed beautifully on the tablecloth. Once a little one went missing. Sure enough two programmes on kids who went missing, all were quite safe though thank goodness. Oh dear, they don't forget do they? I didn't rate too high in the nanny stakes I'm afraid.

I have around a string of pretty blue beads. Every time they've caught my eye I have remembered a film, RANDOM HARVEST, acted by the same artist as MRS MINIVER with RONALD COLMAN. He plays a First World War soldier who suffered from shell shock. The same thing happened to my father so I should have known that they would use it somehow.

After a time of perfect happiness he goes out one day and just as my father did, loses his memory. The three years of happiness a blank. She finds him and one day to make him remember says poignantly, holding a string of BLUE BEADS up to her face…

"HE SAID THEY WERE THE COLOUR OF MY EYES…"

That week of the blue beads I found the book of the film.

Thinking about my former employer and how kind and understanding she was and wondering if she had been in the original plans as others have, instantly A CHRISTMAS CAROL caught my eye. It was UPSIDE DOWN, I don't think she was in the original plans as others have been but instead, a wonderful, loving, useful

RANDOM HARVEST.

Soon after getting the idea a song came along,

♪ HOORAY FOR HOLLYWOOD. ♪

You're telling me…

I had to keep leaving this to turn off a dripping tap. It was the BATH and OH DEAR! It is turning GREEN! Hadn't noticed that before, we must have copper pipes then.

NAT collects stage biographies. One day he went to mention an old music hall artist he was reading up on when he suddenly couldn't remember his name. (There we go again). Then he caught sight of an old antique postcard photo I had put on the piano after finding it in a box of 'odds and ends' and exclaimed...

"THERE IT IS THAT'S HIM, GEORGE ARLISS."

I said, "DO YOU OFTEN HAVE COINCIDENCE NAT?"

He replied, "ALL THE TIME. IT'S A WAY OF LIFE."

The night before auction day I was playing a recording of OLD MUSIC HALL SONGS. In the middle the music breaks off giving way to OH FOR THE WINGS OF A DOVE.

The next day at the auction, along came the lorry with our little brother's name on the side. (The auction being in the open air). I pulled up in the car park to see that the next car to me had a slogan written in the back window, 'THANK GOD FOR JESUS'. Sure enough there he was.

NAT has taken up embroidery as his many interests do have to be easy on his physical strength and I was ASTONISHED. On his jacket were a KINGFISHER, DAISIES, JESUS along with a DOVE OF PEACE. Things that have been mentioned in these records, nearly all in the same stitch as my mother's picture. HONEYSUCKLE that my father had reminded me of in one of his stories. (All too many to include) was growing out of his pocket. I said, "HONEYSUCKLE NAT?" and he replied, "YES, THATS WHERE I KEEP THE FERTILISER..."

There was a religious badge, on it a CANDLE STICK! That's it! NAT is the CANDLESTICK MAKER.

I was moved and could suddenly see why people do need a little time to GET USED TO THE LIGHT.

He had been made to park his car so that it was facing a different direction than usual. As he was sitting in the driving seat the SUNRAYS came again in the sky, like on the day of the silver lining, they were exactly in front of him. I said, "CAN

YOU SEE THE SUNRAYS NAT?" he answered, "OF COURSE."

"OH THANK GOD FOR JESUS."

As I write music is playing, an old number...

 ITS RAINING SUNBEAMS

a song that refers to a WEATHER BUREAU.

ALEX has just come in, and tapped his BAROMETER.

There is a lovely story of ALEX PEGASUS and a BAROMETER but no room to include it here. Perhaps a sequel can be written one day. We shall have to see what transpires.

After I had written this, I had second thoughts about whether I had made the right decision to exclude it, so I have left it to the editors to decide if there is room for just one more story.

I bid for a BAROMETER. Got it for FIFTY PENCE. The arrow was set at CHANGE. ALEX was delighted with it.

He is so stalwart and kind, and has hardly missed a day's work in all the time I have known him, as long as he can have a regular routine he is happy, no amount of bad weather will worry him though he didn't like change. As long as he can have a regular lifestyle, he is happy, but he was an inveterate 'stay at home'.

As a young boy, he lived in the tucked away village, a typically countryside life working on a farm and cycling into the little town for recreation.

At nineteen years old he was called up and quickly sent into the AIRBOURNE service where he was found to be adept at radio. I think the multi-heritage showing up even then, but that was his first experience of change. A D-DAY GLIDER and the capture of the PEGASUS BRIDGE, then known as the

ORNE BRIDGE, was not exactly the most comfortable way to see the world for the first time.

After his de-mob, he came home from a trip to the seaside only to find his father had joined the Dimension people. Its not surprising that for him travel was always associated with depression.

Last year he read the BRIGADOON STORY and does know now that his poor fellow soldiers who didn't come back weren't left in the cold ground after all.

One day I brought a book of photographs of LONDON TREASURES. Soon after he announced that he was going off to LONDON with a friend. He came home with the most marvellous photos. He is a fabulous photographer, although he has had no training like lots of multi-heritage people, has multi-capabilities.

The pictures of LONDON TREASURES and THE HOUSEHOLD CAVALRY made a very interesting collection along with a FLYING DISPLAY he got to as well. He had a terrific time. His fear of change completely gone.

One morning on his CB radio, (his codename PEGASUS), "HELLO RED LEADER, COME IN, RED LEADER."

"HELLO RED LEADER, HELLO RED LEADER," and a reference to ADAM twice that afternoon a television play and the dialogue went:

"HELLO RED LEADER, HELLO RED LEADER."

"PEGASUS HAS TAKEN OFF."

At first ALEX's take-off was a very gentle process so it is appropriate that the aircraft in the play were microlight planes. He has since travelled the length and breadth of ENGLAND and WALES and we have many lovely photographs to remind us.

CLIFF and ADAM are suspect with the influence of this story, but to try to write it all would overcrowd the stories.

The following entry to this journal was made later.

On the day of the sunbeams NAT was swinging an elegant CANE, like the ones that Victorian gentlemen used to carry.

At the time he was taking singing lessons and his fine voice in the style of HOWARD KEEL went well with his black hair, dazzling smile, and FANCY TOPPED CANE.

Sometime later, NAT joined the people in the Dimension, so of course like all of them, his identity came in as can be expected in several ways. One took the form of 'SHOWBOAT' the musical. In it the dazzling smile and fine voice of HOWARD KEEL and the FANCY TOPPED CANE, and would you believe it? THE FULL NAME OF OUR LITTLE BROTHER IS IN THE CAPTIONS...

Once when riding along I noticed nearly every car that passed me was BLUE. The next day the same thing happened. BLUE as you will remember is associated with ADELE (BLUE DOLLY story). In the original notes I had said that "I wonder if her mother would be finding all her groceries had blue wrappings or something of that sort." When I got home after seeing the BLUE cars, every label, eggbox, and wrapping on my shopping, was BLUE!

One day I had to take the bike to be repaired. All the cars parked outside the garage were BLUE, with the ones that passed by they altogether made a dozen. It probably takes a dozen Dimension people to organise a dodge like that. Until then I hadn't realised how organised they have to be. Of course to get all those cars on the road at the same time would mean a lot of research as the drivers welfare has to be studied carefully.

At the beginning of this experience when my darling friends were in the backlog stage, I got silly about hanging the washing on the line. The fear that someone would be passing by and say something hurtful was only in my own mind but for ages I took it to the launderette.

At the garage the box fell off the bike; all my clothes were scattered. A little boy helped scoop them up so I asked him to HOLD ON to it, while I strapped it on again.

In the workshop sitting on a shelf was a BLUE DOLLY, its caption HEAVEN SENT. A young lady arrived wearing a BLUE JACKET. The name of her motor scooter COMFORT. I went for a walk while the bike was being seen to, relieved that DAVID didn't have to remove the box; and wandered into a churchyard. A little space had been kept for children's graves, one had fresh flowers and was dated thirty-five years ago.

That evening ALEX came in with a free bottle of COMFORT washing conditioner someone had given him.

One morning I arrived at the auction town a bit earlier than usual, all the same quite a few people were about. They seemed to be sort of dodging each other and nearly bumping into me and just missing each other round corners and saying 'sorry'. It had happened several times before so it dawned on me that it was too frequent to be accident.

There were children all around too as it was half term. In a shop a little boy ran into me with a <u>bump</u>. He wasn't hurt but the pattern was by then obvious, but why? I wondered.

ALEX had asked me to get some CARROT SEEDS from the gardening centre and said "LOOK OUT FOR THOSE GIANT ONES THAT COME FROM HOLLAND." A lorry parked just outside my window with the name just framed 'WINDMILL CAKES'. They do that a lot with commercial vehicles as they have to turn just outside our house. I had no idea what the WINDMILL CAKES were meaning though.

We saw a little boy so fair. I said, "ALL HE NEEDS IS A PAIR OF CLOGS THEN HE'D LOOK A PROPER LITTLE DUTCH BOY."

Someone remarked about how flowers were brought daily from HOLLAND to sell here, reminding me of a show we did with a WINDMILL scene and a crowd of kids in Dutch costume. The song TULIPS FROM AMSTERDAM. They started on about a story of a little boy in history who was said to have put a finger into the hole in a dyke that was holding the flood waters at bay.

ALEX went on quite a bit about his DUTCH SEED. Vegetables began to be prevalent, people talking about them in overheard conversation, all puzzling though.

The next morning after the bumping incident with the little boy, ALEX was looking out of the bedroom window when he said laughingly, "LOOK, THERE'S TWO COPPERS UP THE ROAD AND ONES TURNED ROUND SUDDENLY AND THEY'VE BUMPED INTO EACH OTHER." We were 'tickled pink'. I had said nothing to ALEX about the bumping the day before.

In a jumble sale queue on the day of the bumping I had been fascinated by TWO little babies in their prams both dozing in exactly the same way. There were children catching my eye everywhere.

Of course! Then it dawned, THEY'VE GOT CHILDREN TOO HAVEN'T THEY? And the message?

HOLD ON, HEAVEN SENT COMFORT IS COMING to all, like the people who own the FLOWER, FRUIT AND VEGETABLE SHOP whose baby boy went into the Dimension.

I know it is poignant. If we could try not to cry. They've had so much of it haven't they? Come to think of it though, they are only happy tears after all.

As the weeks went on children's identities came in steadily. In ALEX's gardening paper was a story of a little boy who won the giant vegetable competition who has the same name as one of the Dimension kids. They stuck to the vegetable theme and I got to know when they were around, as people would just be missing me in the street and talking about their CARROTS.

One day I saw little tiny bags of CARROTS in a supermarket. TWO tiny children with their mummy were choosing CARROTS. I said, "CARROTS DARLINGS?"

And they replied, "FOR A DONKEY."

With the gardening paper they were informing us that the kids have joined in the battle to make us know that they are there and it became more obvious as the weeks went by that they were 'HAVING A BALL'.

ALEX has just come in with a bag of spring flower bulbs; they are miniature ones and they've started to shoot. Now what do they mean by that I wonder.

On telly one afternoon a famous pianist was saying that his gift was not of his own making but that it came from 'somewhere'. The beautiful designs that are appearing in the shops now suggest to me that the clever talented people in the Dimension can somehow inspire our minds to create lovelier things than ever before. In a shop were some tiny models of FAIRYTALE CASTLES, like the ones that I have painted for our show scenery. I always put one in every show like a trade mark. They are becoming numerous like the GOLDEN WEDDING CLOCKS. The possibility is high that they are the product of the coordination that is growing with the multi-heritage becoming more common. Every single person has some natural ability in some direction and the Dimension people can help us make the most of our capability, and direct us into finding out what that is. But they have emphasised that they can't give us help to develop a skill if we haven't got a tendency in the first place. They know better than we do what our natural gifts are.

They say that we often don't realise our own potential and so before long many of us will be quite surprised to discover new directions that we haven't noticed before. How else could the curtain have gone up on our shows?

As a child I had no intention of studying in any way, with the call of the lanes and woods there was no question of practising the piano more than was absolutely necessary. How could such stuff compare with a cycle ride uphill and downdale, always somewhere new to discover. Even now it is bliss to walk through wind and rain which does puzzle me a bit as rough weather must surely have been a nuisance to my gypsy forebears. But I was perfectly confident that I would one day, and simply took it for granted, be part of this entertainment that is so important to the world. How the dickens I was going to do that I had no idea, but the story of how the dreams or a little harum scarum 'LONG AGO AND FAR AWAY, came true, will have to wait until another time. Mind you, the

Dimension kids have made no secret of what they think of my piano playing!

All those things like the LANTERN-LIKE ORCHID HOLDER and MOTHERS DAY CARD, why that could have been designed by my mother, HEAVENS! I bet it was and FRED ASTAIRE, is probably at this very moment telling someone;

 "LET' FACE THE MUSIC AND DANCE."

Twenty-four hours after I had written that, 'be blowed' if FOLLOW THE FLEET didn't come up on the telly, the film in which FRED sings and dances to that song. In it a girl named CONNIE who owns a SAILING SHIP.

The afternoon of the film I had brought home a smart DRESS SHIRT all pristine in its wrappings; FRED is wearing one in the LET'S FACE THE MUSIC dance.

A couple of days later I came across a video of the film in a charity shop.

And not long after this they got into KNIGHTS!

KING ARTHUR'S KNIGHTS and his round table, MEDIEVAL KNIGHTS of the time of RICHARD THE LIONHEART, THE ROBIN HOOD ERA and up-to-date MODERN NEW YEAR'S HONOURS KNIGHTS. Why, they even got FRED into a SUIT OF ARMOUR!

Shortly after, they got into the story of CINDERELLA and how her FAIRY GODMOTHER tells us that, sooner or later OUR CASTLES WILL RISE, meaning that for all of us... happiness will come.

And the document says...

...THE VISION OF MUSICIANS AND WRITERS OF FAIRYTALES AND SONGS AND DANCES WITH WHICH HE CHOSE TO WORK...

I'm beginning to see what it means...

Out with her dogs one day, NANCY found an old coin. After cleaning it she found it to be an old SIXPENCE.

When we were off jumbling I asked her for something to eat. I hadn't been able to go home for a meal so she gave me some RYE CRISPBREAD (slimming stuff). Don't miss a trick do they? She said it was sesame seed and called my attention to the fact that this is BIRDSEED. I shoved it in my POCKET. On returning home noted on the side a book "A SONG OF SIXPENCE."

The following Monday out on the road I noticed dead birds. They had been showing up regularly, big black ones. After some time it struck me that they were always in the same area. It was sometime before I realised this though. In my box of odds that day were TWO of those things that we put in the centre of a PIE to keep the pastry up and later TWO white aprons like the ones I used to wear in the big house when I was a MAID. In another box was a pack of OLD MAID CARDS. (What cheek! Less of the old if you don't mind). The theme persisted as these things do. JILL kept on about how people should take care with pesticides, and being sure to read the directions on the tin properly. The BLACKBIRDS became too frequent to be accidental and I began to gather that there was more behind it. I must say I was still very slow in getting what they were on about. Then, quite suddenly it dawned; "TELL THE RSPCA MAN (I see him regularly) ABOUT THE BLACKBIRDS; SOMEONE HAS NOT READ THE LABEL ON THEIR PESTICIDE TIN."

Unfortunately, by the time I had got the hang of the message it was too late to send one to the RSPCA for examination. Never mind, that was a long time ago. I've improved since then.

The old rhyme goes…

SING A SONG OF SIXPENCE, A POCKET FULL OF RYE
FOUR AND TWENTY BLACKBIRDS BAKED IN A PIE
WHEN THE PIE WAS OPENED, THE BIRDS BEGAN
TO SING
WASN'T THAT A DAINTY DISH TO SET BEFORE
THE KING.
THE KING WAS IN HIS COUNTING HOUSE
COUNTING OUT HIS MONEY
THE QUEEN WAS IN THE PARLOUR, EATING BREAD
AND HONEY
THE MAID WAS IN THE GARDEN, HANGING OUT
THE CLOTHES
ALONG CAME A BLACKBIRD AND PECKED OFF HER
NOSE.

Even though I was sure that my friends were over their backlog reactions I was still nervous about going into the garden in case someone came along who hadn't recovered.

The SIXPENCE STORY turned up at the same time as the BROKEN DISHES, but I didn't have to pay for the dishes and I didn't have to hang out the clothes either. The lady in the BIG HOUSE used to wash her own smalls and use the laundry so they wanted me to REVERSE something.

"THERE'S NO NEED TO BE AFRAID OF HANGING OUT THE CLOTHES. NO ONE'S GOING TO PECK YOUR NOSE OFF."

I decided to trust the Dimension people and the first time hanging stuff on the washing line, a lovely neighbour passed by who had read the BRIGADOON STORY. She stopped to have a happy chat. All was as it had been before. Her backlog which had been quite severe, was over.

ALEX saves up all his little coins in a bottle and was made to count them all in the front room so with a reference to THE KINGS NEW SUIT that took care of the king. JILL was telling us how nourishing HONEY was and full of vitamins so that saw to the honey but the QUEEN was missing.

Later ALEX came in holding up a record sleeve. On it a beautiful FAIRYTALE CASTLE. I said, "It's lovely dear but we've already got a copy of THE THREE ELIZABETHS."

This is a piece of music representing three English Queens ELIZABETH the FIRST (Good Queen Bess) THE QUEEN MOTHER and our present QUEEN ELIZABETH the SECOND. It was some time before I realised that THE KINGS NEW SUIT <u>does</u> refer to the QUEEN. Like a game of TIDDLY WINKS they keep on trying.

I was made to see FIVE MAIL VANS all in a row. On their sides a ROYAL CROWN and noticed that the typewriter in my use, is called ROYAL and the other spare one IMPERIAL. I had sent the manuscript sample to BLOOMSBURY in LONDON by post and wondered DOES THE QUEEN HAVE SOMETHING TO DO WITH THE MANUSCRIPT?

The same theme kept turning up; a story of THE QUEEN MOTHER when she went back to a place in LONDON that had been bombed during the war. She actually remembered a CAT that she had seen, having gone there after the air raids over forty-five years before.

Currently playing is the music from

 MERRIE ENGLAND

In it a reference to the nursery rhyme...

PUSSY CAT PUSSY CAT WHERE HAVE YOU BEEN
I'VE BEEN TO LONDON TO SEE THE QUEEN.

I thought, associations with the QUEEN must have something to do with the manuscript? It came back with the words,

THIS IS NOT OUR FIELD.

I expect you're getting this now. The QUEEN went to the cat, not the CAT to the QUEEN (bless her heart) so we have to REVERSE something. Mind you, I did have trouble with my reverses in the beginning but we'll all improve with practise. Of course I sent the manuscript off again.

The whole meaning of this story was obscure. The possibility is high that I missed some of the clues so have found that when I do, they will often come back with the story and start all over again. We are indeed a game of TIDDLY WINKS.

One market day I was looking for something for a birthday present when I spotted a MUSIC BOX. The man on the stall wound it up to demonstrate that it played the theme from LOVE STORY. It was like a tiny CHEST OF DRAWERS. I kept an open mind and went off to a café. Been in there umpteen times but had never noticed before that the proprietor's name was the same as the MUSIC BOX young man in the Dimension.

One day soon after, there was a FIRESCREEN for sale. It had a CRINOLINE LADY embroidered on it but was grubby. Just as I decided that its condition wasn't good enough, I heard a young girl say "I'M GOING TO BID FOR THAT BOX OF CLOTHES, ITS GOT SOME OLD DRAWERS, YOU KNOW, THE ONES WITH THE LONG LEGS." I didn't bid for the firescreen. It went for ONE POUND and immediately realised that it was a BLOOMER, as I could have washed it.

It was days before I remembered THE CRINOLINE LADY was wearing DRAWERS with the long legs. They wanted me to get the words BLOOMERS and DRAWERS when later at the jumble sale someone held up a pair of OLD FASHIONED DRAWERS laughing. Then I began to notice that when DRAWERS were mentioned, the MUSIC BOX young man was going to draw attention to the fact that his mother was going to be there. One day there were BLACK ONES and she didn't turn up, so I quickly caught on to what he was saying.

The code became more sophisticated as time went on, but they have said that I must not try to put it all in this book as, like a language manual, we must always start with stuff that is easy to understand until we get used to it. But there is a point I must include. When the black drawers turned up they were saying "NEGATIVE his mother would be there," but when they want to cancel out a NEGATIVE message, they follow it up with another NEGATIVE thing so that it cancels (or negatives) the previous one. They will make me hear some unhappy remark in overheard conversation or other things like when a child will screech. They can know when a child is likely to be overtired or fretful and move me within earshot.

They use this system if I am contemplating buying something that is not good value or warn me if I haven't got enough money in my purse. There is no need for alarm if these overheard remarks in conversation are very depressing. They can make use of everything. The kids are often behind a lot of this.

When there is no external situation that they can use to counteract (negative) a negative thing, a depressing word will go through my head. I can only pick up single words, very rarely two or three, unlike DORIS, who could hear sentences, but it is useful to the code at times. They say that it took ten years to train one person and if I don't teach others what I have learned they are

KEEPING A DOG AND BARKING THEMSELVES.

As my gypsy friend has been prone to remark a couple of times recently – and we must 'take note' when things repeat.

As I was checking this page I picked up a faulty pen. The ink escaped and got onto the page and all over my hands. I knew that I had got something wrong, so duly checked carefully but could find nothing seriously amiss with the writing I went on using the faulty pen and began to wonder if they wanted to leave the story out altogether, but that didn't seem to make sense either. I got up from the divan thing I was sitting on to wash the black stuff from my hands when it dawned. I had been laid up for a day or two with a back problem. It was better that day for the first time but I had been sitting in a bad position, as I realised to my cost, when I got up to wash my hands.

I think the Dimension people must have been trying to do it for centuries and that would explain some of the old superstitions. I bet all the DP groups are chuffed to bits now that someone has pulled it off at last.

Just as I was finishing this ALEX interrupted with a lovely GREEN lettuce he had grown. I said, "Shush I'm trying to concentrate," and he replied, "KNICKERS!"

Poor ALEX. It was the loveliest GREENEST lettuce I had ever seen so I told him so. About this time loads of things seemed to be GREEN, just as had happened once before.

One morning I bought from a store in a jumble town some of those biscuits called HOB NOBS. I put them in a corner at the jumble sale with some other things and went to look at another stall. When I returned, my biscuits had been put out on a table and sold by mistake. I went back to the store and asked for another packet of the HOB NOB type cookies.

On the way home saw a shop called HOB NOBS and after that the expression NOBS for 'you know what'. I was baffled.

The DRAWERS persisted as only our drawers can. CHESTS OF DRAWERS, KNICKERS, BLOOMERS the lot. One jumble morning there were UNDIES GALORE; PINK, BLUE, YELLOW, GREEN, those nylon ones that we used to buy from MARKS AND SPARKS remember? Very pretty. They were all lined up along the table. Someone said 'LIKE A RAINBOW'.

I sat down for a cup of coffee when a lady came up to me and said, "ARE YOU THE PERSON WHO HAS BEEN HAVING COINCIDENCE?" and explained that she'd had such lovely experiences and went on to say that her son-in-law in the Dimension had told her how to change a plug. She was puzzled why people didn't understand her though and said, "I FEEL SO SORRY FOR THE REST OF THE WORLD THAT DOESN'T KNOW." (As we all know we must always get a qualified person to check an electric plug if we have had no experience).

Later we had a rainstorm. In between showers the sun was shining so I took a cup of coffee and sat on the doorstep to wait for the postman. ELLA passed by and I remarked, "I'M WAITING FOR A RAINBOW ELLA." But no rainbow materialised until I caught sight of a washing line and there it was; PINK, BLUE and MAUVE. PRETTY COLOURS all in a row.

RAINBOW KNICKERS!

Very resourceful these DP people aren't they? And that's got to be the understatement of the year. As I said earlier, they have never let me forget it.

Oh dear hysterics! I was a bit apprehensive wondering if I would have to remove this, when a telly dialogue went...

"DON'T GET YOUR KNICKERS IN A KNOT."

The QUEEN came up again. Lovely films reviewing her troops. THE QUEEN MOTHER too, frequently. Soon after TOPS became prevalent. I had a little WOODEN TOP in the kitchen DRAWER, the TOP one, then a group of WOODEN TOPS in a second-hand shop window. TOPS all the time but I was not impressed. (Think I would have learned by now wouldn't you?) Then the QUEEN again and references to someone named QUEENIE. People kept talking about BISCUITS and the term 'TAKES THE BISCUIT'. This is an expression for astonishing.

One day, falling asleep while the telly was on, I was suddenly wakened by the remark,

"ITS IN THE TOP DRAWER."

I thought, is the manuscript sample something to do with the QUEEN?

THE NOBS, THE TOPS, THE DRAWERS, OF COURSE!

THE QUEEN IS TOP DRAWER!

THE MANUSCRIPT HAS GONE INTO THE TOP DRAWER.

Meaning, that it has gone into the reading file of the TOP CLASS PUBLISHER because it

'TAKES THE BISCUIT'.

HOB NOB is an English term for mixing with the upper class.

A couple of days later there was a letter to say that the publisher was interested in the manuscript sample and wanted to see the rest. Opening it the clock struck TWELVE NOON.

One morning while at the kitchen sink a word went through my head quite clearly,

'ASTRONOMY'.

Shortly after the code came up to warn me that it was going to come back. They used the song

♪   PICK YOURSELF UP   ♪

Wondering if I could bear the disappointment they used another,

♪ WHEN YOU WISH UPON A STAR,   the words were so comforting.   ♪

♪   LIKE A BOLT FROM THE BLUE,
    FATE STEPS IN AND SEES YOU THRU   ♪

It was true, the manuscript came back within an hour of the code 'tip off'.

I was very unhappy. The day after it was my birthday. At the market I picked up an old birthday card. On it the words 'TO MY DEAR DAUGHTER' so the pain was eased.

That evening, when I was walking down the road after dark, there was an amazing SHOOTING STAR. It swept across the sky like something from a Disney film. It could have been a satellite burning out, as that may have been easier to predict. After all they probably <u>can</u> see through our telescopes.

So that's why they used "WHEN YOU WISH UPON A STAR"

I felt immediately better and as time went by they explained that the right time would come when the manuscript will be accepted and that I must be patient for the time being.

There were more clues to bring comfort, among them a piece of music entitled

I UNDERSTAND JUST HOW YOU FEEL. ♪

performed by FREDDIE and the DREAMERS.

Mr father's name is FRED and his companions are the people in the 'dream' (the dreamers). There are other clues but too many to include.

Up until the twentieth century and even later in England we had a big CLASS division in the way we lived. Peasantry and class never mixed socially on any large scale so that we always married partners from our own social background.

If a housemaid had loved the young man from the big house and had a baby, it would be unthinkable for it to be brought up in the 'class' home. Of course, I know there would have been the odd exception, but generally the babies from such relationships, although probably provided for sometimes, would be brought up in the simpler lifestyle.

The Dimension people tell us that our minds couldn't develop as well as the multi-heritage mind could and this is turning out to be positive. All the people I have come across since, who have been like DORIS STOKES and a friend who is HALF SPANISH and HALF IRISH and can read the manuscript without the backlog problem, are what is generally known as PSYCHIC. I know that the class system provided us with some very clever and beautiful people. Would we and our allies have won the war without it?

In the Victorian era upper class people used to go to the opera and although earlier Shakespeare did write comedies, generally in the nineteenth century the stage stuff was often sad and tragic. Although the music was beautiful, the opera would not have been a lot of help in getting laughter in crowds strong. I know that there would have been exceptions. I am speaking of the majority of stage productions, before the MUSIC HALL and the GILBERT and SULLIVAN comic stuff came along.

When our joy level is raised it increases our awareness of the Dimension people. In the MUSIC HALL DAYS the seats in the gallery were cheap enough for a poor person to go and it is possible that the Dimension people found that when they were in a laughing crowd they were able to make themselves heard by the subconscious mind.

At the time I was writing this NAT gave me a book on the history of pantomime. I see that it has been with us for a very long time. In the book is a picture of a family waiting for a train after a panto outing. They are clearly definitely not poor people, as the children look very elaborately dressed. It is probable that the psychic tendency was among the poorer people. I think the multi-heritage was more likely to be in a Gay Nineties audiences than earlier in the century and why haven't I thought of this before? On the night that I wrote the document I had spent the day with crowds of happy excited people at the OLDE TYME STREET FAYRE. They all must have had a higher positive level afterwards and I would have been more receptive. That does remind us that the country folk did have the FAIRS and travelling theatre companies so a little recreation must have been had occasionally, even for them but this would have been rare.

Life for everyone was sad though when you think of the child mortality rate and just going to the dentist was an ordeal. No one in any walk of life was very far from tragedy to be able to get their JOY level up enough for the Dimension people to be able to get themselves heard on any vast scale. There may have been one prevailing factor though, which could have alleviated some of it.

With the way we used to marry people from our own backgrounds, the chances were higher than they have been in recent years of marrying OUR right ones as we only mixed with our own class and the lifestyle needs would be more likely to match. It is not surprising that in the past couple of decades this has been a little 'thrown'. The Dimension people do say though that we will be more coordinated and our chances of finding happiness much more likely in the future as the help and organising influence is getting more powerful all the time.

The document says

NO ONE WILL HAVE ANY PROBLEM FINDING HAPPINESS IN TIME BUT, AND THIS IS IMPORTANT, WE HAVE TO WAIT UNTIL THE WORLD'S BACKLOG HAS BURNED OUT...

This could mean that the muddles that we are experiencing now could be explained by the fact that the 'info' that is coming from books and telly programmes telling us that we are eternal, is beginning to be understood, and for a time we can't function at our best until our backlog has all gone.

The Dimension people do emphasise the importance of this book not becoming too long, so I have to be careful not to get carried away. But it could be important for us to grasp some simple things.

I'm sure that beautiful music must raise our positive level and anything that we personally enjoy doing must do the same, but there is a high possibility that when we are in a crowd of laughing people we somehow generate a power that has a healing influence. The time will come when they are able to teach us about this.

When we were rehearsing for our musical shows my friends would lose the tiredness after a hard day's work. The more they laughed, the less tired they became. Laughter seemed to be like a magical healing power and I'm sure that in time they will be able to give us more information.

The higher our misery level is the harder it is for the Dimension people to be able to guide us. I think that when we experience a severe backlog we can't hear them at all. As the Dimension build up their workforce they will be able to help us anyway by influencing others around us as they did in the dentists.

COMPASSION on the part of someone can dissolve the effect of a severe backlog when large groups of people pray together, they are conveying COMPASSION probably. The more we understand this the more powerful the Dimension people's love can be. I am sure that in time they will be able to give us a logical explanation of how it is that some people can actually heal others. I have seen this happen. I do have some ideas that may explain it, but I need to wait to see if some more clues turn up, which they probably will.

One could argue that if they could organise me to be on the road that the young motorcyclist was on, couldn't they have stopped the accident in the first place? The explanation is simple. They would be only too well aware that the boy rides too fast around those lanes. If he has a high misery level then no matter how loud the Dimension people tried to shout out at him to "Watch out! Slow down," even with the intelligence that his age group may well have now, he would not have been able to hear them. Many young people nowadays may have a high misery level when one thinks of how the media is bombarding them with frightening things. Young people are unlikely as a general thing to admit that they are afraid, so it is not surprising to me that they are seeking escape. I don't know how long it will take but sooner or later co-ordination will come and the Dimension people will be able to save us from these things. It is only our ignorance of how it all works that is the cause of so much suffering. There are many programmes that are comforting and educational. People who live on their own would be lost without them, so I am not criticising television generally. I believe <u>no</u> <u>one</u> is to blame for the unfortunate presentations that have a frightening effect. If a presenter has to go into the 'thick of it' and into danger to report tragic and depressing news stories, which these courageous people have to do, how can we send help if we don't see it?

When editors have to work on tragic and sad stories it can't do anything else but lower his (or her) JOY level. Unless there is something to raise it again, it is likely to affect their choice of following presentations.

Sooner or later peace of mind will come to everyone and the tendency will change.

The identities go back to about 1915. I think VAN BIENE may have left them and gone full circle but I haven't in this case got anything too solid to substantiate this. They kept on about him a lot with CAVALIERA RUSTICANA and a reference to him too a little while ago published in a book as recently as 1988; THE GREAT CELLOISTS, so they definitely want to tell us something important about him. I wasn't as efficient in deciphering the code then as I am now, so I expect I could have missed clues as well.

They conveniently saw to it that another book was put in one of my boxes and in it a reference to reincarnation. It contained stories of people who insisted that their dead babies were sent back to them. One was very interesting, well they all were, but this was of a chappie who lost TWO little girls and insisted that the second two were the original little ones. The address where he lives is in the road where I went at first to find the BED and BREAKFAST place on the BRIGADOON TRIP.

So much has come correct that they predicted, that now I have no trouble in believing them. The code becomes more informative each week, so in time they will be able to develop it enough to give us more information as time goes on. Meanwhile,

WE'RE NOT COMPLAINING ARE WE?

Some time ago I met a lovely girl who is called a MEDIUM and she said that it all tallies with what she has found out.

In the war when people were transisting in great numbers there must have been confusion and loneliness. So much misery must have been generated, but now this is all CHANGING. Every time someone joins them the whole thing is different.

More people are there to explain how it's all working and happiness and optimism are stopping the misery that was so prevalent before. There has always been people there to explain I expect, but now I think the groups are becoming more organised thanks to the people who have gone before who have had the determination to make us understand enough to last out until their numbers grew stronger and so more powerful.

Just after writing this a psychologist came up on television and he said that when people realise that their consciousness is permanent they become, in time, compassionate and kind and I think he used the word TOLERANT. Pity we had no video at the time.

The telly coverage one evening was the anniversary of the DAMBUSTERS, the RAF SQUADRON which dropped the bouncing bomb. The next day a friend said he had just got a painting of the DAMBUSTERS' PLANE and A SPITFIRE. The DAMBUSTERS' MARCH MUSIC coming up too.

At a fair the following week we were at a coconut shy when a SPITFIRE swooped down directly over our heads. It was the same one as in my friend's painting. Later at a garden party, I met a lady who told me her husband had been A FIGHTER PILOT in the Battle of Britain. For days after his name came up all over repeatedly and in my box that week was a record of the BATTLE OF BRITAIN theme, along with the DAMBUSTERS' MARCH. As I was playing it, just as the music gave a kind of fanfare, a low-flying plane swooped over the house to synchronise. It was then that I wept for the first time; that it should take people so long to accept the Dimension people. After all the patience and struggle they have had to go through to make us know that they are there. BUT THAT WAS SOME TIME AGO.

The main reason for this being, that when our worst fears are stopped we go into REVERSE, not realising until now that the uncomfortable feeling is only TEMPORARY and NORMAL.

In the document it says...

'CROSSES HAVE HAD TO BE BORNE'. As well as human sacrifice. I think this is all alluding to the fact that people had to be organised to marry their wrong ones in the hopes that a group of multi-heritage babies would be born, with all the right receiving capability in their minds so that out of all of them, one would have the right genes to be able to pick up the code. Also, the patience they must have had to hand over the plan from generation to generation and keep on and on trying to attract our attention. They were aware of our need for conservation problems during the thirties, even earlier, and the danger we were getting into, so the misery they must have felt in not being able to make us understand must have been a 'cross' in itself. Later they were able to give us more information and with it the realisation that ALL IN TIME WILL BE WELL and how all tears will pass and only laughter can remain.

Immediately after I had written the SPITFIRE story, I settled down for a rest and a film of AMY JOHNSON came on. Across the screen go SPITFIRES. In it someone refers to a FLYING VISIT.

The day before I wrote this story I met the lady who was married to the BATTLE OF BRITAIN PILOT. It was the first time I'd seen her since the garden party. I was on my way to find a card to send to my little grandsons to tell them that we could go on a trip soon, like we did on the day we saw the SPITFIRE swoop down at the fair. As usual I waited for guidance on what kind of card to choose. Then I saw the picturecard that would be suitable. It was of a SPITFIRE and, of course, I had my instructions on what the next story must be.

That morning I had tried on a smart white coat at the jumble sale. I didn't buy it, as it was out of date. AMY was wearing the identical one in the old film. They do it all the time. Even now though, I miss a lot.

One evening I was thinking I'M MISSING HALF OF IT, just at the same time in a play the dialogue went "YOU'VE MISSED A BIT THERE."

As I write, a film is synchronising and someone is saying to a girl called CONNIE, "SEE WHAT I MEAN?"

When I checked back over this chapter I saw that there was no story attached to the DAMBUSTERS. Shortly after, I heard of a retired RAF chappie who had taken part in the DAMBUSTERS' RAID. It could be that they want me to mention the film which was shown of the inventor of the BOUNCING BOMB which was used in the raid and who worked patiently over and over again to get it ready in time, and the inventor of the Wellington Bomber that CLIFF flew.

Later they came up with the explanation for why they wanted to draw our attention to people like this.

ALEX has just come in and said "Good programme on tonight, you know what's his name? The fellow who invented the jet engine."

Footnote: There are books written by AIR CHIEF MARSHALL, LORD DOWDING who was the architect of the BATTLE OF BRITAIN which make references to young pilots who were killed.

One does talk of a young RAF boy who flies with an aircrew so as to guide them. Although Lord Dowding's books are very old, they can still be found in English libraries. They are entitled, MANY MANSIONS and LYCH GATE.

The DAM BUSTERS piano music turned up, on it was a picture of the actor who was in the same outfit as ALEX at the capture of the PEGASUS BRIDGE. The composer was in the same orchestra that my father played in, but not at the same time. And so they keep going...

In a BOTANICAL MAGAZINE I saw a wonderful story of how botanists had carefully bred seeds that were descended from the plants that were brought here on the old sailing ships in the last century from the TROPICS. The little plants were getting along nicely in the south of England in large numbers and as that was some time ago they probably had been taken back to their homeland and planted in the depleted RAINFORESTS as they grow very quickly I gather.

I always put my keys in the greenhouse. One day people started to talk about their keys – in the street and at a jumble sale. In a café a lady was saying that she forgot her keys so she sat in the GREENHOUSE. Soon after the song HIGH HOPES came up and it goes THERE GOES ANOTHER RUBBER TREE PLANT. Sure enough, two films in one day about RUBBER TREES. I was really flummoxed with that one as I couldn't see what KEYS had to do with RUBBER TREES.

Soon after in a gardening book was a picture of THOUSANDS of CLOCHES; individual little glass things to put over plants. Greenhouses kept continually coming in as well and little faces peeping out of those old fashioned CLOCHE HATS that we wore in the twenties, together with the song that goes,

PEOPLE, PEOPLE WHO NEED PEOPLE and the PEOPLE TREE and WHAT A WONDERFUL WORLD. OF COURSE! KEY PEOPLE! That's it, KEY PEOPLE!

Then the name MITCHELL all the time. MITCHELL? OF COURSE, the SPITFIRE. R. J. MITCHELL INVENTED THE SPITFIRE! In the thirties or earlier, he was intensely sure that the country was in danger, so, although he was ill, he still kept on getting the spitfire ready and we all know how it saved us.

What the KEYS and CLOCHES were meaning was that all over the world there are people like R. J. MITCHELL who from their school days, or even earlier, have been sought out. Just like little plants under glass and the TROPICAL RUBBER TREES in a greenhouse, with their happiness, health and safety watched over carefully because, like R, J, MITCHELL, they have a vital role to play in CONSERVATION, SCIENCE and MEDICINE.

Every time someone joins them, the work force, the power becomes stronger in the Dimension. They are more intelligent than we are and can inspire our subconscious minds with the IDEAS for saving everything and have no problem with working as a team because they have no misery. When we are free from misery we can't be anything else but constructive in all we do. The world's recovery can't come in five minutes but they say that if we look closely we will see signs already of hope for the future. It is like the SEA SNAIL that is mentioned in a book illustrated by the WILDLIFE ARTIST who stayed with us, or a BALLOON, slowly drifting all over the world. Every month the numbers of happy people in the Dimension will increase and with them POSITIVE POWER.

Soon after I had written this I heard of a friend who has been offered a wonderful opportunity in CONSERVATION. Oh! That probably explains the reference to 'ACTION STATIONS' in the Brigadoon story.

Here we go again, I found it under the piano lid when I wrote this story. Must have been there for years.

One day I decided to leave the bike behind and coach ride. It went around the remote villages and winding lanes for miles. I could see in the distance the hill where I had sung
♪ THE SOUND OF MUSIC. ♪ The route took us past the houses where a young lady had lived who had taken part in a professional version of that show and is singing on one of the records that I play. She is in the Dimension now.

As we rode I was silently singing a tune from the show but not the same one as I had sung before. Over and over it went in my mind.

♪ BUT SOMEWHERE IN MY YOUTH OR CHILDHOOD
   I MUST HAVE DONE SOMETHING GOOD ♪

Odd really, also as I thought, totally inappropriate as no way could I think of ANYTHING good that could be attributed to my childhood. That is why I have always had compassion for youngsters who get things wrong, having been there too. I thought surely MARIA'S song would be more appropriate from that show?

♪ SHE'S ALWAYS LATE FOR EVERYTHING
   EXCEPT FOR EVERY MEAL...
   MARIA'S NOT AN ASSET TO THE ABBEY

I knew that if the song persisted it had some meaning though.

As we turned a corner a car came along too fast. How we missed it I don't know, talk about a close shave!

The same thing had happened a couple of days before too. As we carried on our way a beautiful RAINBOW appeared, perfect, complete, like the first one in the field. On our left the hill – clear and lovely but the rainbow was on the opposite side of the bus; I noticed this so didn't get too excited although it was gorgeous. Then, as we rounded a bend slightly, the hill reflected in the bus window and the rainbow appeared to be encircling it. GOSH! It was perfect, like out of a fairytale book. The song persisted and persisted.

 SOMEWHERE IN MY YOUTH OR CHILDHOOD
I MUST HAVE DONE SOMETHING GOOD

On my return a film and in it a pram was running away. It registered a couple of days later when another film portrayed the same thing. Someone catches the pram just in time. OF COURSE! Then I remembered, as a kid I saw a pram racing down the hill. I caught it seconds away from disaster. After the film several others, all with this 'just in time' theme. BUT ALL WILL BE WELL, no need to worry, they say. WE ARE IN TIME to save everything, but
BABY, IT WAS CLOSE!

What I did notice at meetings of psychic people was that comfort and accuracy would come in 'leaps and bounds' and then there would be an identity that no one knew. The pattern was pretty consistent and odd when so many other things would be accurate. It could be though that this inaccurate information is deliberate on the part of the Dimension people so that our joy capacity isn't overloaded to an uncomfortable level and so we understand about the Dimension gradually. The need for this is going to fade in time as so many of us are being 'broken in' now.

We can see why the meetings were sometimes unpopular as mediums must have often have stopped fears and then the 'backlog' set in next day bringing strange and uncomfortable feelings.

Sometimes when the psychic people end their session they can be quite tired. I've found too that if I relax and concentrate on the code propped up on a pillow like when we do deep relaxation exercises, it's more comfortable to get up slowly and recover gradually as one can feel quite dazed for a short while. This is normal and can be handled perfectly once we understand it. Actually lying flat is usually part of relaxation but I find the pillow more comfortable as one hasn't so far to get up. A little gentle hand rubbing and toe wiggling can help speed up the recovery though.

I choose early in the morning to review all the films and events of the previous day, as at that time of day there is little chance of somebody knocking on the door. When this has happened during the times of full relaxation, I have jumped up quickly and found that I would become as 'giddy as a goose'. (Although what is there about geese that they are called giddy? All the ones I've come across have been quite bright). Never having suffered from this before I was quite alarmed, but when I checked it out with medical people, they explained that when we are very relaxed all our system is slowed down. If we jump up quickly it takes a little while for it to get going again, so the giddiness was perfectly normal and completely avoidable once we realise that we must just get ourselves going again very slowly. One medical friend said, 'Just count ten'. What about a phone? Just turn it off for the time one needs not to be disturbed. I expect this is all common sense to the average person, but I have to make allowances for the fact that I may not be the only person in the world who can be as THICK AS TWO SHORT PLANKS' (although we've probably got to go a long way before we find one).

There has to be a logical explanation for why I can remember events and films of the previous day in a relaxed state and the opposite seemed to apply when I used intense concentration to play the piano and I got the burning face thing and the faster metabolism of the Brigadoon trip. Somehow to intensify my ability to play the piano or write, like after the return from the OLD TYME FAYRE – they have to raise my metabolism, but when I only have to listen and not do anything physical it works better to be totally relaxed. The piano intensity lessened after a time as I became a little more proficient. I daresay that eventually they will be able to explain these things more fully. One thing that they have made clear is that they never push us beyond our limit and they know exactly how much effort we can withstand. So when I was quite dazed from struggling to play the piano I was subconsciously aware of DAD saying

"STOP and RELAX."

They have made it quite clear that they can't take us over. If this was possible they would have been able to let us know that they were there centuries ago. They can only guide us. Once we understand the reason for these sometimes uncomfortable sensations they cease to be a problem.

As the years go by the need to be silent will go too as we become more adept at noticing the code. Some people have had so little practise at being so GLAD that they could sing with JOY, but they will be surprised at how quickly they can learn.

UNCLE GEORGE'S DRINKING SONG AGAIN and references to CHAMPAGNE and CELEBRATION.

JILL had a record. She turned it over several times, on it a picture of the SEA. The word TURN and TERN came up a lot. A recording of TURNER LAYTON the stage artist too. They use everything they can think of and are not fussy about the phonetic spelling.

THE SUMMERTIME THEME kept coming up as the year went on and references in a CHRISTIAN magazine to positive influence growing and the words on the front

'THE TIDE IS TURNING.'

One day in a café were rows and rows of mugs with names on. There must have been a HUNDRED at least, no exaggeration. As I was looking at them a clock struck TWELVE NOON loud and clear. There were a few people whose identity still hadn't come – GLADYS, sister to TONY and JOY another friend. That day, someone whom I see week after week said, 'HELLO GLADYS', (she got my name wrong) and shortly after I saw a sign – 'JOY'S RESTAURANT'. The same afternoon of the MUGS, exactly as I was going into my gate a HUGE passenger AIRCRAFT flew slowly past the house and almost straight away another big transporter went across the back. Both of them low, like a FLYPAST.

When I got into the house I put the telly on. A film was about to start about a chap who was some sort of ANGEL and was supposed to

'BLOW HIS HORN AT MIDNIGHT'.

It was too far into the story to get the whole plot, but he was in the throes of trying to BLOW HIS HORN before midnight struck and I think the idea was something to do with JUDGEMENT DAY. Anyway he didn't get to blow it, thank goodness. I switched channels and a girl was singing a song about BLOWING A HORN AT MIDNIGHT. The same theme.

I was reminded of a remark that was made on television about the progressive mess that the world was getting into. It was 'IT'S FOUR MINUTES TO MIDNIGHT'. The NOON and MIDNIGHT theme was backed up again, along with THE GOOD OLD SUMMERTIME, and that was MIDSUMMER, the day of the MUGS and the BIG PASSENGER AIRCRAFT. The MUGS had names on, rows and rows of them... but the chap in the film THE ANGEL, never DID GET TO BLOW THE HORN although it was a close thing.

I think the GOOD OLD SUMMERTIME songs were referring to the time when their numbers would increase to the HALFWAY MARK so that fifty percent of people in the Dimension were involved in the big plan to organise the world's affairs in politics and conservation – people who have had experience in these things and go on being interested in them and influencing them now.

The plans to get a book written accelerated in the last few years and it does look like there were people in the TUCKED AWAY VILLAGE who were organised to buy the houses there so that it would be easier to keep an eye on them when they transisted. It was the sort of people they were that makes me suspicious. Their interests were CONSERVATION, MUSIC, POLITICS and MEDICINE. Another knew ROYALTY and another SHOW BUSINESS. When a well-known politician came in with his identity he used a BOX OF HEALTH FOOD PILLS and a lady who knew ROYALTY was happy with JAM LABELS (as well as other clues.)

The class distinctions are missing from the Dimension, not that this lot had any anyway. The concentration of people who were experienced in matters that are of the highest importance to world affairs was far higher than the average.

One day Alex brought home a book on the history of the little TUCKED AWAY VILLAGE. In it was a picture of the house where a chappie had lived who was in intelligence in the war as a CODE BREAKER.

The accent on the GOOD OLD SUMMERTIME kept going. Obviously they wanted us to understand that something of importance was going to happen then.

Immediately after writing this, I decided to pack up and watch a film. It told of a man who was comforted by the girl he loved who was in the Dimension. The film was based on a story that had been written by a lady who used to visit the TUCKED AWAY VILLAGE. I think it could be a reminder that I had made no mention of WRITERS who lived there.

The world can't do anything else but recover eventually as the POSITIVE INFLUENCE has OUTNUMBERED THE UNHAPPY people in the Dimension and the whole operation is under control – that was three years before his final writing. No wonder they were talking of CELEBRATION.

One day while playing a record of MERRIE ENGLAND (this is a musical based on the days of GOOD QUEEN BESS), it coincided with the ARMADA's four hundredth anniversary and the south of England celebrated with a repeat of the BONFIRES that were lit at intervals over the country to warn us that the ARMADA of Spanish ships was on its way to invade us. It was defeated and after turning back had to go round our island before returning to its homeland. I don't know why this was, perhaps it was something to do with the TIDES.

My dear old dog DANNY transisted. I nervously wondered if they would be able to tell me anything about him as he was the first animal to transist since this experience. The next day in bed reading about dogs I heard two dogs barking. They sounded like two friends of his who lived quite two fields away. Had it been JOSH's little dog I wouldn't have noticed it the same. Didn't pay much attention and thought if it means anything, they will follow it up with something else. I pulled a piece of paper out from under the music stool where it had got stuck under the leg. It was the picture of a KINGFISHER that I had torn from a book and had been on the mantelshelf when SHEILA's letter came with the Conservation Trust picture. Sure enough, in the post again a letter from her enclosing photos she had taken of old DANNY when on their visit. In the photo was a big toy dog in the background – they always like to DOUBLE things when they can. The flash had reflected in his eyes so they just looked like two white stars or jewels, like it does when we look into the camera sometimes with specs.

It must be confusing for transisted animals at first, as they must wonder why we aren't noticing them, but they get used to it and it must be easier if there is anyone already there that they can recognise, so DANNY will have remembered BELLE his previous owner. They must be able to transmit an image of themselves somehow as they can see each other just as we do.

On the day he left us I went off jumbling as ALEX wanted to be alone for a little while. The jumble sale was for the POPPY appeal. In the queue someone with a dog on a lead called out the name BELLE. Inside the hall, on the windowsill there was a sprig of gypsy heather. It seemed to be all references to my father that afternoon, so I wondered where my mother was.

I managed to be very brave as I knew without a shadow of a doubt that DANNY would be all right and it must be so depressing for the animals in the Dimension to see us crying so much. Of course his AUNTIE and my mother would have stayed with ALEX with others, to reduce his distress with their compassion and BELLE would have taken DANNY away so that he didn't see his sadness, so I think BELLE and DANNY were in the queue at the jumble sale that day.

A few days later I went to a sale organised by my own loving friends. Someone had decided to get rid of a whole collection of DOG ornaments so there were 'umpteen' all over. At the auction HARRY said, "WHAT AM I BID FOR A DOG CAGE? JUST RIGHT TO TAKE THE DOG TO THE VET."

I ended up with a box of odds. Inside was an ornament of DOUBLE DOGS and the EYES WERE MADE OF SPARKING JEWELS. They sparkled just like the eyes in the photo when they caught the flash.

"DANNY CAN SEE YOU."

Some people mentioned the mushrooms and the fields so I was being reminded to go down where I used to with him. Sure, he'd be coming down there with me to relive memories too.

Soon after I overheard a conversation in a village hall. A lady was saying that she had lost her little doggie and had just seen one like it. She said he had PUT HIS PAW UP TO HER JUST LIKE HER OWN LITTLE ONE USED TO and added "I FEEL SO SAD."

I could say nothing but so hoped that she would put two and two together so that the 'PENNY WOULD DROP' as the saying goes, as that is the sort of thing they organise when checking in an identity for us.

Not long before, the Dimension people had indicated that the manuscript must be held back for a while. They used the music THE FOUR SEASONS and GEORGE FORMBY singing a happy song that synchronised

WE'RE ON THE BEAT,

from the film, SPARE A COPPER. Which was relevant later.

This could have been because other books were coming onto the market telling us about the Dimension People and letting the light in, and it was important that this one must have the right timing. They said that for the time being (and the seasons came round twice before the 'tip off' came to start sending it again) I must be content to wait and say nothing more to anyone.

They all have their own particular code and one young lady who had lovely long legs used those telly advertisements for tights. One has a clock face, the hands are going round minute by minute and are a pair of long legs clothed in glamorous tights. When it is repeated I know that she is saying something. In one case the remark that they wished to be recalled was when she used to say…

"THERE'S A REASON FOR EVERYTHING."

The work they must have done to prepare all the plays and films so that they would follow each one shows how patiently they have had to wait for the results as some of the films were made in the thirties. They must have been planning this way back and were influencing the script writers long ago.

It was when the lady with the clock tights had come up again and taking a rest from working on the book, I put the telly on, a film was about to start. In the cast list was the full name of the lady who was the mother of the baby who was in the pram the day it was saved when I was a child.

The film dialogue that was meant to be noticed was;

"ALL IN GOOD TIME, MY DEAR."

They went on to reassure me that they could 'MAKE TIME FLY' for which I was truly thankful.

Immediately after writing this the young husband of the lady with the tights came in. He said,

"CAN'T STOP, NO TIME. THIS IS ONLY A FLYING VISIT."

ALEX asked me why I was laughing. I replied, "Can't tell you now, but will one day," after which, when SHEILA and ROSE asked how the book was getting on, I had to answer, "Just fine," and leave it at that. How puzzling the silence must have been for them.

The great day came when they said it was right to send the book again. It came back with much more encouragement than ever before. I think that in the meantime publishers had received submissions with similar themes and this would have got them used to it so that it was easier to read and assimilate having been 'broken in', so to speak.

One day while in the library looking up publishers addresses, I heard a mother looking for books, she read aloud to her little girl,

"DICKORY DICKORY DOCK, THE MOUSE RAN UP THE CLOCK."

I wouldn't have noticed so much if a friend called DICK hadn't been there too, looking at a map and studying with his magnifying glass the SEA.

It wasn't long after that the Dimension people got into OLD SAILING SHIPS again and so often they were coming into harbour. (DOCK).

Every single day from then on a clock would strike. These ranged from BIG BEN on radio and telly ads; to our own TOWN CLOCK.

Meanwhile the identities kept up a steady stream. PADRE JONES who was VICAR at the CHURCH in the TUCKED AWAY VILLAGE was able to tell us that he knew all about those ARUM LILLIES he had given us to give to my mother in hospital. We thought they were too formal so we hid them in a cupboard and forgot them. This was when I lived with ROSE.

It was one of those things that she and I talked of when we met again. PADRE was once in charge of a little church in ROMANIA where he knew QUEEN MARIE long ago. He had personal letters and photos of her, so I know it was true. I believe he was the inspiration behind the little book I found in which there was the information about the ROMANIES being taken for slaves in ROMANIA.

During the time PADRE's identity was coming in earlier in the year. I'd taken off to an evening jumble and parked the bike outside a church. As I looked up at the door, the street lighting seemed to outline the magnificence of its gothic stonework. The sky was clear and sparkling with millions of stars and was so beautiful I was still thinking of it when I got home and put the tape recorder on. Immediately the song THE HOLY CITY. The words tell of 'I SEE A TEMPLE THERE' and go on to tell of a dream that one day all will be well with the world.

After writing this I stopped for a rest and put the telly on when a dialogue went "THE HOLY CITY IS ONCE MORE IN CHRISTIAN HANDS," and went on to talk of ARMISTICE to the strains of the song THERE'S A LONG LONG TRAIL, A WINDING meaning I think that the NEW JERUSALEM that the song refers to will take them a little time.

Some children were playing with a YO-YO. This is a TOP that is manoeuvred up and down a piece of string, and very expert they were too! Its success depends on balance. The YO-YOs were repeated another day by more children who knocked on my door to show me.

At the cheese market I asked for three quarters of a pound. She cut a piece which weighed exactly right and gave me ONE PENNY in change. Someone called her name, "MARGERY."

Meanwhile a telly game came up. The presenter remarked about all three contestants being called John. In a film shortly after there were THREE JOHNS in the captions all together. The MARGERY name again too.

In the health food shop they were short staffed so we had to wait for quite a while. I had time to study all the pots of natural medicines on the shelf. Some were called NEW ERA. When we arrived at the counter the assistant apologised and did the same thing as MARGERY did with the weight, and gave me ONE PENNY in change.

I have some lovely friends who travel like gypsies do. They are keen on conservation, natural medicines and organic food. Their concern for the earth has led them to peaceful campaigns against cruelty to farm animals and the positive things all so important to our future. The hippies as they were dubbed were responsible for knocking out the class distinctions in England in the seventies and so many of their children will have the new intelligence as they must be multi-heritage.

There was a trailer for sale. Some people were standing on both ends, among them a beautiful MOTHER-TO-BE dressed in the traveller style. The far ones stepped off so it started to go down on the young girl's side. There was no problem, it just went down taking her with it.

The Dimension people wanted her to represent the FUTURE. They went on to explain that now that the Dimension people are working together on such a big scale they will, in time, be able to 'PHONE IN COMFORT' to our subconscious mind. That when we lose a loved one, we will somehow be able to manage in a way we weren't able to in the past. This will become more powerful as time goes on.

The time will come when future generations will be able to hear the actual voice, but before then the knowledge that they are safe will have come and this is going to start altering our physical health and the decisions we make. For instance, the need to smoke will not be so intense. So much illness will be avoided that way. Doctors in the Dimension will be able to inspire Doctors here with new ideas, as their intelligence is ahead of ours.

Of course, 'ALL WILL TAKE TIME', as they colourfully pointed out 'ROME WASN'T BUILT IN A DAY'.

All the same it isn't going to take hundreds of years either. It just stands to reason doesn't it?

The old rhyme goes
SEE SAW MARGERY DAW
JOHNNY SHALL HAVE A NEW MASTER
HE SHALL HAVE BUT A PENNY A DAY
BECAUSE HE CAN'T WORK ANY FASTER.

I must learn to be patient like in the health food shop queue. THE NEW ERA WILL COME, THE NEW JERUSALEM, when all will know with absolute certainty that we are eternal. They were able to explain why it CAN'T GO ANY FASTER and only here and there can the PENNY DROP for the time being.

The young mother represents the FUTURE and they are telling us that the BALANCE IS ON HER SIDE.
and
THE TIDE IS TURNING
IT IS NO LONGER FOUR MINUTES TO MIDNIGHT
THE ARMADA THAT THREATENED THE WORLD
HAS TURNED BACK
THE DIMENSION IS IN CHRISTIAN HANDS
And WHEN THE MULTI-HERITAGE COMES

THE WORLD WILL HAVE A NEW MASTER.

SNAIL SHELLS kept turning up. I found a huge one in the field. Odd that, it was like those snails that the French use in their cooking. How on earth did it get there? ALEX came in with a bag of SEASHELLS.

I shoved one in my pocket along with a shiny tiny sword, it must have come from some toy. The sword exactly fitted inside the shell. I had once said to the lady in the big house,

"THE WORLD'S MY OYSTER
AND WITH MY SWORD I'LL OPEN IT."

Thinking about it now it could be a fitting slogan for the PEOPLE FROM THE TUCKED AWAY VILLAGE.

The children are playing an essential part. They are far more intelligent that when in this dimension. Whether this is because they can see everything from a clearer view point or whether it is just that their minds are unhampered by anything unconstructive and they are free from any sort of misery. It stands to reason that when <u>our</u> lives are serene, and this is inevitable once we are fully aware of the comfort of knowing that all is well with our loved ones, unhampered as we will be for the first time in mankind's history by the mystery we will then make better decisions. It's just common sense that our own intelligence will improve. Our misery level must get lower just with that problem removed from our minds. The Dimension has always been there first so it stands to reason that their intelligence is going to be better than ours. Even the simplest things will count, for instance, for the first time in my life I've stopped biting my nails as I no longer have misery – the doctors who said that that was a tension symptom had it right. In fact its marvellous when we think just how many things they <u>have</u> got right, in spite of the mystery that people have had to live with.

So much credit must be given to people in history who have been willing to suffer for mankind's sake like the religious martyrs with their teachings of faith. They saved it all because they stopped our misery level enough to keep the balance above the danger level generally. The children are numerous now. DORIS had a wall covered with photographs of children who had been able to contact their parents.

Tiny babies just doze and I think they could be first in line for the 'return trip'. The more excited and interested they are, the more awake they stay. They've explained that they can sleep sometimes. Mind you, the Dimension people do say that with the invention of the TELEVISION and its ability to depress thousands of people in one go, and so lower their joy level on such a vast scale, they had to get their thinking caps on smartish as at the rate it was going, mankind would not have survived till the new mind came naturally. 'BUT ALL WILL BE WELL NOW', they say.

The children grow up so that by the time this book is on sale these original ones will be mature and they will have trained others to take their place before they move on to more grown-up things.

I'm sure that they will be keeping track of the present lot though. The fact that the children mature when in the Dimension has been backed up by psychic people.

Footnote:

The television programmes have begun to come up with some very positive stuff; DANCING ON ICE, SO YOU THINK YOU CAN DANCE, and others like this are filling a lot of television time now, so my optimism that the turning point is not far away is not unfounded. I did laugh, too, at the lovely series of POP STAR TO OPERA STAR, after all, I had said about the OPERA in the early nineteenth century; but this is twenty-first century, people singing it and I was delighted to see that it was the happy songs that got people's votes. I think others will see sooner or later a turning point in the world's affairs. Much to their surprise.

OH I nearly forgot, there was

 OVER THE RAINBOW

as well.

In the beginning the kids used to come in when there were carnations on the café tables. As we progressed they used all sorts of things. One day went to see NAT, he was at church. I was surprised as they organise us so they wouldn't have wasted my time without a reason, no matter how small the reason is, as tiny things count for something too. Sitting on the step I noticed a big CARNATION in a pot. In the breeze it brushed my face.

One day when NANCY was out with her dogs she found a cheque book with a signed cheque in a BREAD bag. She took it to the police station. On her way home the collie found a BREAD ROLL in the litter bin.

About that time NANCY was having a hard time and she couldn't have any sort of little treat. She has a twenty-two (or thereabouts) inch waist and is about five feet, so doesn't suffer, as I do, from a surfeit of cream cakes. A few days after the cheque incident there was a lady at her door holding a box of chocolates and a bunch of CARNATIONS and was so thankful for the cheque book.

Not long after, the baby boy in the Dimension from the FRUIT AND VEGETABLE SHOP was joined by his daddy. Straight away his identity came in. A film so obviously his check in.

When an old friend of ours checked in <u>her</u> identity, she used her surname, the brand of a famous GLOVE FIRM. The advertisement had a picture of a HAND HOLDING A GLOBE. We had sung the song in our shows.

 HE'S GOT THE WHOLE WORLD IN HIS HANDS
HE'S GOT THE LITTLE TINY BABY IN HIS HANDS

And the song IF YOU'RE HAPPY, CLAP YOUR HANDS.

I can now hear the strains coming from the telly of some children singing IF YOU'RE HAPPY AND YOU KNOW IT CLAP YOUR HANDS.

OH DEAR, THEY ARE POINTING OUT THAT I'VE MISSED A BIT OF THE SONG, HAVEN'T I?

The daddy's identity came in for days. In the film they used the other song as well that we had sung and it was in the same order. No mistaking the message of JOY.

The globe has "HEAVEN SCENT" on it and the gloves have tiny faces on each finger.

The kids' WINDMILLS came up frequently afterwards, it's a pity they can't all go in this book.

This entry was made later…

In the original notes I had a lovely little story about a MOUSE. One made his home in our PIANO. At night I used to hear a funny little noise as he ran along the strings.

Everyone laughed and someone referred to the words of a song we had used in CINDERELLA

 A MOUSE WITH CLOGS ON…

From the song A MOUSE LIVED IN A WINDMILL.

I was astonished when his little identity came in when he went into the Dimension. I didn't include it in the book but this must have been disappointing to whoever thought to make one of us leave a door open knowing that some crumbs had been dropped on the floor, (or something of the sort) I bet the kids thought that one up, so I have made amends.

When I got the typewriter out to settle down and retype this, ALEX called me from the sitting room "COME IN HERE QUICKLY OR YOU'LL MISS 'FLOG IT'."

This is an antique programme so I went in to please him but I did want to get on.

The presenter was studying a little automated toy. It was a little band of MICE and one was PLAYING A PIANO.

This second reference to a mice band probably could have been because some people think of mice as negative so to be on the safe side they used two.

Photo courtesy of DUKES of DORCHESTER

Before my experience in SCOTLAND there was a news item on the local telly station about a young boy of thirteen (or fourteen) who was terminally ill and had only a few months to go. He was wearing a peaked cap. He had expressed a wish to ride in a POLICE CONTROL CAR. His wish was granted and the telly news sent a cameraman. The presenter probably didn't want the assignment, poor chap, but the skill in which the young boy handled the situation was still more evidence of the new intelligence that is on its way.

The Dimension people can intensify our memory and even though the programme was only a few minutes, I can remember the lovely face as though it was yesterday. When there was a tragedy on the telly, the identities came up frequently. When more than one was lost they let one identity come in so that we could assume that all were safe. They used the most convenient name, like a young man called CRISP, for instance. So CRISPS came up in conversation or boxes of odds. They always checked something in. After a while they stopped doing this, I think because they know that we will now take it for granted.

I couldn't remember them all though, even if I wrote five books, but the identity of the young boy who rode in the POLICE CAR never came up. I wondered if it was just that we could take it for granted as I had been so impressed by his personality. I did so wish that it would though.

One Friday I went off for a day out on the bus. At a bus stop a boy was wearing a peaked cap – on it a PAIR OF CLAPPING HANDS. I didn't register until a little while later when another boy got on aged about thirteen and wearing the identical cap (it didn't have the hands though). His companion began to whistle. Then the boy in the cap took up the song.

HE'S GOT THE WHOLE WORLD IN HIS HANDS
HE'S GOT THE LITTLE TINY BABY IN HIS HANDS!

Then the bus passed the television studio that the programme came from about the young boy. Waiting on the side of the road was a POLICE TRAFFIC CONTROL CAR.

Two days after, I saw a young boy in a van, the resemblance unmistakeable! HE WAVED HAPPILY TO ME and in my mind I said LOVE YOU TOO DARLING.

The latest record is playing now –

 THREE WISHES.

Now if I'm not mistaken I can guess what the other two are and being the smart young man he is there won't be much we can tell his MUM and DAD.

Last Sunday an old friend whom we haven't seen for ages pulled up outside my gate and asked to see ALEX. He was accompanied by a young boy and was keen to get to know all the kids, being a COPPER. The car was a POLICE TRAFFIC CONTROL CAR.

As I am typing this in the kitchen I can hear the telly in the next room. The programme is THE BILL (English slang for police). When I have been worried and anxious the kids have reminded me frequently 'WE'RE ON THE BEAT, and the answers have come.

The peaked cap became very common later but when this was written there weren't so many about. Also the same thing applied to the MUGS that had the names on. And OH DEAR! It has become fashionable for people to wear their hair tied back like CINDERELLA when the MOUSE took the BLUE RIBBON out of the drawer for the BLUEBIRDS, in the Disney version.

Now doesn't that have a familiar ring?

They want us to notice mirrors.

If someone is talking of some unhappy experience or illness, if a MIRROR is nearby we have to REVERSE the simple warning. They don't have to be reflecting in it as long as one is nearby. If the word REFLECT or REFLECTION is used in conversation this counts as ONE. So when the hill with the rainbow REFLECTED in the bus window they had to counteract the OPPOSITE way round message in some way.

On the day of the ride round the hill I hadn't learned about the MIRRORS so I didn't register as I would now, whether the coach had one or two in my sightline. Two would cancel out the first. I called to mind the time that the hills were reflected in a bus window in the film THE SOUND OF MUSIC so the first reflection cancelled out the REVERSE in the second. There was no rainbow in the film, it was only the hills that were in reverse on the bus ride round where I had sung THE SOUND OF MUSIC that day with such joy.

I have never known them to use a MIRROR to reverse a positive remark and when I have noticed a positive happening like the reflected hills there is always something to counteract the reversal.

The reference to THERE GOES ANOTHER RUBBER TREE PLANT which tells the story of a little ant who eats his way through a RUBBER TREE until it falls, has actually got at first sight, a negative theme. The reference earlier to YOU'VE GOT TO BE CAREFULLY TAUGHT, also has the same tendency so I think that as the first song is from the musical SOUTH PACIFIC where the RUBBER TREE grows, then one negative song will reverse the other.

Also the one that FRED ASTAIRE sings in FOLLOW THE FLEET;

 LET'S FACE THE MUSIC AND DANCE

has an unhappy theme. It bothered me a bit, so I replayed the video which I found shortly after the telly film and the part where FRED is getting ready to go on stage to perform the number.

Just before he was handed the DRESS SHIRT by his Chief Petty Officer friend, FRED had been looking in his MIRROR. The BLUE ROSE story has a MIRROR too and the RED LAMPSHADE one features a REFLECTION, both were followed by explanations but there is no room here to record them (BILL'S big brown jug too.) It is important that the code is not made too complicated, we need to understand the basics, the rest will come with experience.

You can bet on it that your loved ones will want to get 'in on the act' sooner or later. Most of us live busy lives, so do the DPs. Lots of us will be content just to know that they are safe and happy.

The motorbike boys in the Dimension come with me on the bike and the group is becoming enormous, but they have a tremendous amount of work to do. No one is having time to 'sit and stare'. The kids adopted ROLLS for their code so when people start talking continually about BREAD and the BAKER as they are passing in the street or on a bus, or in shops, I know that the kids are on duty and are guarding us.

When they are excited and happy about something they use the song THE MUFFIN MAN THE MUFFIN MAN.

A few days after I heard from BOB I was at the auction when BALLS kept rolling into me. It was the children's half term from school and I didn't register until quite a time after how many times that morning I had been BUMPED with a ball. Our Dimension kids were there as the 'just missing each other' kept going and people said "SO SORRY", far too frequently to be accident. Of course it is hilarious. I have to just laugh out loud sometimes, can't contain it.

I found some BREAD ROLLS still in their wrappers that had been thrown away so I took them home for NANCY'S dogs. She has a COLLIE and a SCOTTIE. The kids' code came up when some children were playing with a teaset that they had found in a box. The Dimension kids use BLUE and WHITE china as their code too, but the story of how they started this is too long to include. They started with DUTCH DELFT. I should have taken more notice on the day of the balls than I did.

After BOB'S visit I was walking by the railway track when a train came along, it made a terrible noise stopping and starting and rocking and rolling. I thought salt pots would be shaking for sure and hoped people in the houses it passed had double glazing. I saw someone with two dogs, they were a SCOTTIE and a COLLIE, further on I passed a house. A lady with a SCOTTIE exactly like the one I had just seen was in the garden, a tin of dog food in her hand. She said…

"I FOUND THIS <u>ROLL</u>ING AROUND IN THE BOOT OF THE CAR."

We had a little chat and when I went back up the road saw the SCOTTIE and the COLLIE again. It was days before I 'twigged' it, even though I had bought a tin of SALT that had <u>rattled</u> and <u>rolled</u> round my top box that day, and NANCY has a SCOTTIE and a COLLIE.

The Dimension kids were responsible for getting me to understand the word ROLL. I was supposed to say in the notes SHAKE RATTLE AND <u>ROLL</u>. (Faggot story remember?) I had missed their word.

I got better at it in time, now they go 'hammer and tongs' as the saying goes. I am sure that if I hold on long enough others will notice these things, then we will be able to all laugh together.

A song came up from a musical

WE NEED A LITTLE XMAS and goes on about

SLICING UP THE FRUIT CAKE AND TINSEL AND THE CHIMNEY.

Xmas had crept up on me, only a few days to go when I realised that I had made no preparations. The notes on the coincidences were taking hours and hours and even then I couldn't keep pace with them. I wrote that I didn't know how the dickens I was going to be ready.

I got some flour and fruit and threw in some eggs and sugar and shoved it in the oven. Couldn't believe my eyes when I went to look – PERFECT! Exactly like KATIE used to send round before she went into the Dimension. All very suspicious!

The house seemed to get itself in order. I was amazed at how quickly all the muddles got sorted. I went off to the supermarket on the afternoon of XMAS EVE and with twenty minutes to go before closing time I remembered that I didn't have any frill to put round the cake.

I ran around the shops but they were all sold out and with FIVE minutes left, returned to the supermarket. A little girl bumped me with a baby buggy and as I turned around she did it for the second time. I suddenly had the idea to ask the young lady on the cash desk if she would sell me the GOLD and SILVER tinsel decorating the till. And, for a few pennies she let me have it. It looked marvellous, very shiny and bright. When I got home I played the record my father must have organised for me

♪ THE GOLD AND SILVER WALTZ ♪

I didn't record the GOLD and SILVER STORY so in the newspaper was the headline in HUGE letters, an advertisement for

GOLD AND SILVER

The kids weren't going to let me forget a third time (or was it four times?) The fun and nonsense that they got up to all the rest of the holidays!

WELL! There's no need for me to worry that I can't record it all here, as it's only a matter of time before YOU'LL BE HAVING XMAS GREETINGS OF YOUR OWN. I hope it won't be summertime before you catch on though.

I had sent RON a record. The song went...

 IT'S BEGINNING TO LOOK A LOT LIKE XMAS.
SOON THE BELLS WILL START

And it goes on to refer to a CAROL IN OUR HEARTS, meaning that EVERYONE will have a SONG IN THEIR HEARTS when they know that the Dimension people are there and

SOON THE BELLS WILL START

Every single day since then, XMAS is mentioned by something or someone. As I am correcting this, ALEX has just interrupted to say that he's fixed the Xmas fairy lights.

RAY, the postman, (of the little dog story) does a SANTA CLAUS for a charity organisation. One day he asked me if I could find a HANDBELL in my auction travels. NANCY has a tiny old worlde cottage with funny little staircases and oak beams in the ceiling. One evening we were sitting by her fire with its inglenook when we were examining RAY'S SANTA CLAUS outfit. It was ages before I registered that NANCY was wearing a bright red velvet trouser suit at the time.

In the dining room there was an old-fashioned Victorian fireplace. She couldn't use it as the chimney needed repairing. With the house being four hundred years old, it's not surprising that it is expensive getting it into perfect condition to sell. The rain was coming in the roof around the chimney. Poor NANCY worried stiff about the effect of damp and how she could afford to get it repaired. GLEN was then far away down south and anyway, she didn't want to take his time now that he was working so hard.

One day at a jumble she bought some brass wall lights. I didn't think too much of them, but then I'm not an expert on these things. I took them to an art dealer and he, to my surprise, took the lights for auction. When the day dawned, went off to the sale. Just overhead a BIG PLANE was flying across a clear blue sky. Going into the sale a girl came by eating a BREAD ROLL and was wearing the identical shoes to NANCY'S granddaughter's. The lights that cost one pound got a HUNDRED AND TEN POUNDS!

After she had recovered from the shock, NANCY had to think about how she could get the work done. She was hesitant about alarming GLEN about the chimney as he was working so hard at building up a new life bricklaying, singing in a ROCK BAND and PLAYING GUITAR, so she didn't want anything to interrupt that.

She was sitting in the armchair by the fire when NANCY noticed an advert in the weekly paper. It was for CHIMNEY REPAIRS. Just after she noticed a newspaper on the floor, the sports page uppermost and the headline shot out at her 'COME

ON GLEN'. So she decided to tell him about the damp after all, to find that for two weeks during the Christmas holidays he would have no work to do as his firm was closing down. So GLEN said he would come home for a couple of days.

One evening on the telly someone was talking about selling FIREPLACES and TWO references to MUGS. So I thought BETTER RING NANCY to see what's up. She said "SO GLAD YOU RANG CON. I'M LONGING TO TELL YOU, GLEN HAS DONE THE CHIMNEY TODAY. WE'VE JUST LIT A FIRE. IT'S SMASHING." She was so excited, all anxiety over the damp gone.

The current record is going

BY THE FIRESIDE

This was recorded by JESSIE MATTHEWS who was on the same bill as NANCY when she was in the travelling theatre.

The clock continued to strike each day – on the television, in books, in the town, unfailingly. After a time the clock is followed by BELLS. Often the clock first and then sooner or later during the day BELLS – church bells, hand bells. All kinds of bells. And I met DAVID on his way to church; BELL practise.

AUNT DAISY came in with the MIDSUMMER theme again and uses the record of the musical...

 THE BELLS ARE RINGING

When she lived in the city of London, her little flat she shared with UNCLE GEORGE was situated at the top of a high building in an alley. The echoes of every sound could be heard clearly, although they were seven hundred or so steps up and she reassures us that the 'bells really are ringing' when the music goes ALL AROUND THERE'S THE SOUND OF

THE MIDSUMMER'S NIGHT BELLS IN THE AIR ARE RINGING EVERYWHERE.

I CAN HEAR FOOTSTEPS THAT PASS ON THE STREET. ♪

In one song on the record AUNT DAISY is actually reminding me that I owe her daughter-in-law a thank you phone call. All the songs on that record are relevant but along my street can be heard the sound of the ice cream man and his little tinkling tune I'M POPEYE THE SAILOR MAN just as I had finished trimming round a sailing ship photo to include. So hint taken and must resist the temptation to put it all in the book.

Hold on a bit! Mustn't get too enthusiastic with the trimming. A song that should be mentioned from that show could be

♪ JUST IN TIME ♪

From the top of AUNT DAISY'S building could be seen many famous LONDON LANDMARKS. It was only weekdays that I spent there but I'm sure that Sunday must have produced so many church bells. No wonder they are on about

ORANGES AND LEMONS
SAY THE BELLS OF ST CLEMENTS.

The music "DAISY BELL", "TWO ON A TANDEM" and "WE ALL HAVE A SONG IN OUR HEARTS" turned up at this time.

Isn't St Clements the memorial church to the Royal Airforce and to Lord Dowding KEYS GREENHOUSES and SPITFIRES were all over the place again. A lovely film with EROL FLYNN as a captain of a sailing ship in the time of GOOD QUEEN BESS determined to make her see the importance of forming a fleet of ships to fight the AMARDA, that he was sure was out to invade us. With his fellow sailors he got marooned in a swamp and was successful with his sword in hacking his way through a tropical forest out into freedom and light.

RUBBER TREES too and the PEOPLE WHO NEED PEOPLE song going through my head, I had no idea what they were on about but knew it was something for sure.

I got to know the little grandmother. Besides the songs from WILD VIOLETS she uses the old rhyme ONE, TWO, BUCKLE MY SHOE and when the colour PURPLE turns up, I know she has something to say.

It is twelve and a half years since the rainbow in the field. Shortly after writing it up that day, everything started to turn GREEN. We have a lovely friend who is in the Dimension. She had red hair and so often used to wear that colour.

I had written to GERALD, her husband, to say that "LILLY uses GREEN." A couple of days later I saw him sitting in his garden. The entire lot was LAWN. He had turned the whole garden GREEN.

LILLY, ANNA, ROSE, VIC and ALEX had gone to school together in the tucked away village. ALEX said that first CHRISTMAS, "LILLY was a LOVELY GIRL BUT SHE USED ALWAYS TO BE LATE." I had to giggle when her Christmas greeting came in. She left it until halfway through JANUARY!

It also has just dawned on me that LILLY'S GREEN completes the RAINBOW.

DAD'S RED, ADELE'S BLUE, DAISY'S ORANGES AND LEMONS, my MOTHER'S LILAC and GRANDMOTHER'S VIOLET.

Soon after writing this I walked down the lane. It had been raining and 'be blowed' if there wasn't ANOTHER RAINBOW stretching across the same field, beautiful as though it was painted! I met some people who could see it too. It became more lovely and began to DOUBLE like they do.

On my return ALEX came in and said "I BET YOU DIDN'T NOTICE I'VE MOWED THE LAWN."

After this they turned to all things NAUTICAL. References to the COASTGUARD (who influenced RON to go into the NAVY) LIGHTHOUSES and a LIFEBOAT

COXSWAIN who lived near us when we were on the East Coast and how they have to have 'ALL HANDS ON DECK' and so many old SAILING SHIPS in full sail GLIDING CONFIDENTLY INTO THE FUTURE.

The lighthouses reminded me of BILL; it is ages since I wrote his story. But a programme came up with the jockey in his painting. He talked of "getting near the winning post."

Could it be that BILL is saying that a publisher will have ROOM FOR ONE MORE and he will no longer have to keep reminding me, as he often does, to WALK DON'T RUN.

♪   WE ARE SAILING WE ARE SAILING   ♪

Confidently into the FUTURE all in the SAME DIRECTION as the sailing ship in 'TWO YEARS BEFORE THE MAST'. Altogether there were eight.

After I had written this people became obsessed with their carrots. ALEX brought a <u>huge</u> one in and told me I must look out for that giant DUTCH seed again.

In the street there were two young people, one dressed as a DUTCH BOY, his companion as ANDY PANDY, collecting for charity.

I was reminded of the day when I saw the clocks with the faces and how they were like the clock that I had painted for the kitchen in our production of CINDERELLA.

In a supermarket there was a huge consignment of carrots. I'd never seen so many carrots in my life. They kept up the theme day after day, so of course, no doubt about it, the kids were on about <u>something</u>.

On the telly, someone said, "YOU ARE HARD WORK SOMETIMES." This was not said impatiently as they always have understanding for us and know that we will catch on in time as they aren't going to let up until we do.

Some months ago I saw a friend whose son had gone into the Dimension. I longed to tell her of the code, but the Dimension people indicated that I must hold it back for a while. So I told her to "HOLD ON" and "LATER IN THE YEAR WE WILL HAVE A LAUGH TOGETHER." I am now hoping that it will not be long before I can discuss it with her as I see her at the auctions regularly.

Yesterday we talked of the electricity generating WINDMILLS and how they are harmless to the environment and are giving us hope of new ideas to get power from natural sources. I said, "When we see them they are saying

'HOLD ON WE'RE COMING'."

The week before I had found a record and being without glasses I'd asked her to read the title for me. It was SHAKE, RATTLE AND ROLL. Yesterday, to remind me again, a film with the song SHAKE, RATTLE AND ROLL. Of course there has to be a link and I am hoping that I've got this one right.

I said to my friend "IT WON'T BE LONG NOW," meaning that I could give her COMFORT before long and soon after seeing her I overheard a bit of a conversation in the café and the words HEAVEN SENT. I came home with THICK CUT BREAD, by mistake. Could it be that I have left out one of the children's words again? Should it have been HOLD ON WE'RE COMING SOON?

And means

HEAVEN SENT COMFORT IS COMING <u>SOON</u>.

After I had written this, ANNA came in and said about how she had prepared the CARROTS for a church dinner party for FIFTY people.

As I was checking this page ALEX came in and said

"I'VE JUST HEARD THEY ARE TALKING OF PUTTING AN ELECTRICITY GENERATING WINDMILL ON" and he named the farm where I had seen the RAINBOW IN THE FIELD.

And on the BRIGADOON anniversary this year the sun shone like it's never done before on the PICTURE.

Soon after, Carnival time again. The fairground people arrived in each town with the MERRY-GO-ROUNDS and CAROUSELS. One day our bus was held up while a fairground vehicle REVERSED into a FIELD. The weather turned bad. All the same the parades carried on although it was a miracle that they weren't all blown away.

One night decided to walk down to NANCE. She had been wet through twice that day with the dogs so had to give her a hand with their evening walk.

The weather was awful, so had planned to catch a bus back up. As I waited cars came along and swished water all over me. I laughed when the bus didn't come, so started to walk up the hill, scarf blowing away and umbrella inside out, fighting the storm every inch of the way. Even a bit rough for me!

Early next morning woke to a clear sky, two stars shining and a silvery glow on the horizon heralding a full SUNRISE.

Birds were chippering in the garden, reminding me of films recently with references to LARKS and so many people named BILLY. All the leaves had gone and the brilliant light shone on the picture lighting up the embroidered background. A perfect GOLDEN SKY.

The name SOMERFIELD is relevant

ALEX started to fuss about the string that was holding the picture of JESUS. He said he was afraid it would fall. It looked OK to me but to please him I took it down and replaced it with something stronger. When it was put back up it was hanging slightly lower and at the time I was aware that this would alter the sunlight patch on it. I knew though that it was impossible to repeat the framed effect of that first year as the window frames are inches deeper so the panes are smaller.

The book was returned so many times that my faith was beginning to fade. I sleep in the room with the picture and at dawn in the spring I keep the little top window open so that I can hear the birds' chorus.

One day they were silent, not a cheep could I hear. For the first time ever in the morning I opened the casement. Lo and behold! When the dawn sunlight appeared I was astonished to see that the oblong of light exactly fitted the picture. The figure central and quite beautiful. I thought, surely it must mean something special after all. Why hadn't I ever opened the casement before? I photographed it and saw that the name of the town where it was processed is a SHIPPING DOCK.

Could it be that my SAILING SHIP is coming into PORT, and will there be others to share the PRECIOUS LOAD.

At the same time a very old schoolgirl's book turned up. Because of copyright integrity I cannot include a picture. In it was depicted a piece of music and included in the title was ME

These books were an identity check in. They have the full name of a friend in them, whose name is JOHN and is part of the SEE-SAW MARGERY DAW STORY

Note TWO MARGERYS.

♪ THESE ARE A FEW OF MY FAVOURITE THINGS ♪

Can't put them all in. If we did we would be the size of the ENCYCLOPAEDIA BRITANNICA and we would need a lorry to carry it around. This lot don't believe in doing anything by halves do they?

A lovely book turned up recently about the QUEEN MOTHER, entitled CROWN JEWEL. It is published by BLOOMSBURY. I took it to a bookshop to be sold and when I called in later found it was gone.

In the telly episode of CORONATION STREET, a young lady said that her cat was missing. It turned up again and this is one of those times when I didn't see the connection for a few days, so I wish I could be absolutely sure that I have remembered the dialogue correctly. I think it went,

"WHERE HAVE YOU BEEN?"

Very shortly, almost simultaneously, the EASTENDERS had a cat missing too. This is an English series that is like CORONATION STREET shown several times a week and is set in the EAST END of LONDON. They too used the expression, "WHERE HAVE YOU BEEN?" when it returned.

There are always hardworking and colourful people at the market town. Overhearing a conversation in the shop, I pricked up my ears as you can imagine.

"THE QUEEN BE A-COMIN' ON A VISIT," and the old farmer named the ABBEY TOWN.

About this time an advertisement appeared. It featured a tiny dancer, the resemblance to NANCY striking. She ran and danced merrily over the ROOFTOPS and CHIMNEY POTS and was dressed in a PUSSY CAT costume.

I forgot it though, when a couple of days later I went down to see her but found her out. Next day I said "WHERE'D YOU GET TO NANCE?"

She replied, "I'VE BEEN TO SEE THE QUEEN."

When a play came on I didn't realise even when someone was bidding at an auction and said,

"THIS IS MY FIELD."

HEAVENS! I remember now PANDY, (ANDY PANDY, THE BLACK AND WHITE CAT) he went missing too, only to return safe and sound later. How could anyone be so slow? I deserve to eat THICK CUT BREAD for the rest of my life.

The PUSSY CAT, PUSSY CAT, WHERE HAVE YOU BEEN? story. THE QUEEN IS THE MANUSCRIPT! And could be someone's FIELD! That will explain the influx of TIDDLY WINKS games that turned up at that time. There were other clues too, too numerous to mention like SHOOTING STARS and trips to DISNEYLAND.

At the moment ALEX is playing his taped music,

BIRDS FLY OVER THE RAINBOW
OH WHY OH WHY CAN'T I?

And would you believe it,

NO REQUEST IS TOO EXTREME
WHEN YOU WISH UPON A STAR
AS DREAMERS DO

Followed up with

AT LAST

IS 'BETHLEHEM' IN SIGHT FOR THE LITTLE DONKEY?

and will her dreams that the manuscript will be accepted, come true?

The great day came when the letter arrived to say that the publisher was interested in the manuscript sample and wanted to see more.

At six o'clock the next morning, I turned the bedside lamp on, scarcely daring to believe it could be true and read the letter again. The lamp was standing against a little bevelled mirror, the reflection must have caused a prism (is that the right word, I wonder?), and stretching right across the page was a RAINBOW.

I knew then that the book would be accepted, as if I was going to be disappointed, there is no way the DP's would have let me hold the letter in that position. When the manuscript was posted I remembered a story I should have included so decided to take it.

On the day that I had arranged to take the manuscript to London, ordered a taxi to take me to the bus. Our taxi service is run by such kind people and I have never known them to be anything else but strictly on time. I don't know how they do it, but that morning PETER turned up too early. I had fifteen minutes to wait. I didn't mind, of course, but was surprised as he had never done that before. Actually he probably was a bit surprised himself but if he ever gets to read this, he will have the explanation.

As I waited for the bus a beautiful RAINBOW formed. It was a perfect bow complete from end to end. Had PETER been on time, I would have missed it.

When I arrived in London, I found helpful people all the way. I was handed a map and noticed the name of the area where my father had lived and with his famous tutor VAN BEINE, had studied his cello.

I recalled the recent offering of EASTENDERS where MINTY was looking at an old film called THE BROKEN MELODY. The title of the musical theatre production that made VAN BEINE famous. I had said to ALEX, "What on earth is he doing in EASTENDERS, our story is going back to 1915 for heavens sake," so we laughed, as you can imagine.

The film was repeated in the telly play THE LANDGIRLS in which there was a Cockney girl called Connie.

I was wondering why the film was shown twice, but now realise that the title of the film was sad so they had to show it twice, so that the negative could be reversed. When I wrote to the BBC to ask where they got it from, they so kindly said 'AMAZON', are we into TROPICAL PLANTS again? I thought.

Their reply had for its logo that little map that they show at the beginning of their programme, and I thought of Uncle George's ♪ OLD FATHER THAMES ♪ song.

I looked at the map that I had been handed in London when it dawned on me, no wonder they had kept on about RUBBER TREES, SPITFIRES, KEYS and GREENHOUSES!

The publishers who's destiny it is to bring this *important* story to the world is in the DOCK area and must be within the sound of Aunt Daisie's LONDON BELLS. I knew then that CONNIE'S SAILING SHIP had indeed come into harbour.

The stories went on coming in – SNOW WHITE, JACK'S BEANSTALK, ALADDIN, BOY BLUE, A LITTLE DOG LAUGHED TO SEE SUCH FUN, CINDERELLA AND A POLICEMAN'S BALL and many more.

We have a stunning friend, so kind, nothing is too much trouble for him. He has a habit lately of turning up suddenly when help is needed and seems to appear from nowhere as he did on the day of the SEAGULLS. Totally unaware of how attractive he is, LUKE too was once in a vicious circle. Just as simply, his problem was explained as was GLEN'S. He 'walks tall' now and has gone on to make his life a success.

What Supermen they have had to be to recover and remain the lovely people they are in spite of all they have been through.

I can see from my window the POSTBOX – children are playing by it in big groups these days. They have a YO-YO craze again and are part of the Dimension kids' efforts to tell me that a letter from the publisher will be coming soon. They used a story too of POSTMAN PAT AND HIS MISSING BLACK AND WHITE CAT who came in out of the fog, to tell me.

When I was at last able to discuss it with her SHEILA had said, having written books of her own, "Its an ever continuing story, how can you end it?"

As I write ALEX is playing a song that was the opening number to a show that LUKE stage managed for us.

♪ LET THE PEOPLE SING ♪

I know SUPERMAN that's it, SUPERMAN, he'll do.

Until now, never in the whole of mankind's history have we been able to know exactly what happens when this section of life ends. But for people in history who were willing to suffer for our sake we wouldn't have been in time to save it all. We still haven't got the whole explanation of how the power works that keeps us going, but you can bet your life they'll think of some way to tell us all we need to know.

JILL is an expert in astrology. I call her STAR as she is one and no mistake. Other young people came out into the light besides LUKE, each time understanding the misery theory and their heredity. I was not wholly in accord with JILL that ASTROLOGY would be an important part of our future, but as time went on, I was forced to change my ideas as so many of her personality assessments became more and more accurate.

Outside her house one night with my little grandson (the one in the POPPY story), when he exclaimed,

"COR! LOOK AT ALL THOSE STARS NAN, THERE'S MILLIONS."

I replied, "YES DARLING," and thought

HOW CAN THEY NOT BE PART OF US IN SOME WAY?

As the new knowledge comes, gradually at first, then the CHAIN REACTION OF JOY WILL SPIN EVERYWHERE AROUND THE WORLD, WITH TOTAL PEACE OF MIND, THERE WILL BE NO PROBLEM THAT MANKIND CANNOT SOLVE TO SURVIVE BECAUSE HE WILL BE

SUPERMAN

Epilogue over page

Epilogue

One fine day in June, the MIDSUMMER sun was shining when the post arrived with the manuscript after my proofreading for my final check. It was still months before it was complete and I never did overcome the typing, but the day dawned when the last page was put in. Feeling the strain, I decided to catch a bus, a long long, journey somewhere new would be the answer.

On the way we stopped at a village displaying a poster for a "FESTIVAL OF BELLS". As the buses run through there every hour I alighted, thinking that there would be just enough time.

The church was made beautiful with floral displays depicting all the London churches that are mentioned in the nursery rhyme ORANGES AND LEMONS to celebrate the refurbishment of the bells that after many years now ring out merrily.

Then I remembered the date, it was BRIGADOON DAY.

The backlog manifested itself some weeks later. It must have been a subconscious worry over a long period that it wouldn't be accepted as the generated misery(negative) must then be burnt out. The symptoms lasted several days so I checked them out with my doctor who reassured me, and from then on I made a rapid recovery.

Just as I had finished this, the sun was rising, I looked up from my work and the perfect oblong of light was on the PICTURE for the second time. The words of the HOLY CITY came to mind.

 SING FOR THE NIGHT IS O'ER

As time went on hints did seem to come in that could explain a little about how the power works.

In one of JILL'S new age books I read of KIRLIAN PHOTOGRAPHY. This apparently is a camera that can photograph an AURA that surrounds people and I believe all living things. It is like a glow that becomes strong when we are happy and less so when we are miserable. This must be the power that we generate when a lot of people are together in a JOY situation. It may be the explanation for why we are suddenly healed at a religious gathering sometimes, and where the strength comes to complete lengthy FUN RUNS. When one thinks of how many finish the course it is remarkable. Many people who have taken part have talked of a MAGICAL ATMOSPHERE during the London Marathon. So if there is anything in this then the opposite must apply and so concentrating on negative things, (which is difficult to avoid when our joy level is low), we are likely to be more sensitive to aches and pains.

If we can get into a crowd of happy people enjoying the same things that we do, it is highly possible that we will feel better. I can see why we haven't been able to fully take advantage of this healing simplicity as the backlog will come on sooner or later, either after a prolonged spell of loneliness, or if physical pain is relieved, as it can be when we come into this healing power that comes with large groups of happy people. Sometimes we can wake up feeling worse than we did before, not realising that it is only TEMPORARY. During this time we can't hear the subconscious healing voice of our loved ones in the Dimension, like we've switched off our radios, although they can transmit comfort through other people around us. We only have to wait for the battery charge to burn out which it will and the improvement that we have gained from our experience of a JOY generating situation will return.

Once we understand what is happening to us the period of backlog will be uncomfortable but harmless because we won't recharge it with fear. When our JOY level is at its highest point the Dimension people can make themselves heard by our subconscious mind and give us inner peace. Without subconscious worry our body can get on with the business of correcting itself.

They are getting their workforce built up now and so we may very well hear of more people who eventually feel better once the effects of the backlog can be fully understood.

We know that this isn't the whole story of the power but DORIS spoke of EARTH ENERGIES. I don't know much about these but before a sequel to this is begun (whoever writes it, may not be myself), I hope a lot more information that can connect the AURA with how our personalities carry on as they obviously do, will be available.

Also I hope that they will be able to explain how it is that some people have been able to be aware of the Dimension people even when they have great distress. The ANGEL OF MONS that is talked about in the First World War when a lot of soldiers saw the figure in the sky comforting them is an example. Their misery level must have been full up to the brim but there would have been a lot of soldiers in the Dimension by then to stand SHOULDER TO SHOULDER to convey the compassionate power to overcome it.

I wonder if modern day awareness in times of distress could be influenced by our tranquilising medication too? If we just hold on I am sure they will give us ALL the answers eventually.

When the understanding does come of how the power works, which it will, I don't see any reason, just like in the fairy tales of old, why the world shouldn't live

HAPPILY EVER AFTER

Please continue over the page for an important announcement...

ACKNOWLEDGEMENTS

I wish at this point, to thank my wonderful son
for his support without which this book could
not have been got off the ground. Also my
precious daughter-in-law, who aids and abets
him and myself in everything that is important to
us.

The bells certainly rang the day she came into
our lives

Also I give my grateful thanks to the AUSTIN &
MACAULEY editors for their courage in
launching such an unusual project and for their
COMPASSION so that we can replace our
tears with a

SONG IN OUR HEARTS